WHY EMPLOYEES FAIL TO MEET PERFORMANCE EXPECTATIONS

&

HOW TO FIX THE PROBLEM

WHY EMPLOYEES FAIL TO MEET PERFORMANCE EXPECTATIONS

&

HOW TO FIX THE PROBLEM

VERNON L. WILLIAMS

Empowerment Publishers
Columbia, Maryland

Library of Congress Cataloging-in-Publication Data

Williams, Vernon L.

Why Employees Fail to Meet Performance Expectations & How
to Fix the Problem / Vernon L. Williams

Includes bibliographical references and index.
ISBN 0-9777338-0-7

Published by Empowerment Publishers

This book is available at special quantity discounts to use as premiums and
sales promotions, or for use in corporate or government training programs.
For more information please visit www.vernonwilliams.net.

OTHER BOOKS BY VERNON L. WILLIAMS

- *Paddle Your Own Boat: 10 Rules that Guarantee Career Success*

- *425 Ways to Stretch Your $$$$*

Available at www.vernonwilliams.net.

Dedication

With love and affection, I dedicate this book to my parents, the late Louis and Viana Williams. They not only stressed the importance of a solid education, but also worked tirelessly to make it a reality for all eight of their children.

Acknowledgements

I wish to thank my wife, Gayle, for her excellent job of proofreading and for being a loving and supporting sounding board throughout this project.

CONTENTS

PREFACE

As a front-line supervisor, your job is critical. You are responsible for implementing your organization's mission statement. To do that, your employees must meet performance expectations. But, as I am sure you have learned, they do not always do that. This brings us to three essential questions:

1. Why do your employees fail to meet performance expectations?

2. What are the solutions for getting them on target?

3. How do you implement those solutions?

To effectively answer these questions, rather than focusing on the symptoms, you must begin by identifying the cause of performance failures. Let me tell you a story to illustrate this point.

Little Max was three years old when he woke up one morning feeling unusually warm to the touch. His mother, Phyllis, checked his temperature and it was 101°. She took Max to the pediatrician, who examined him and discovered he had an inner ear infection. He prescribed a 10-day supply of an antibiotic. Phyllis gave Max the antibiotic and the infection left. But it returned after he had taken the last dose. This pattern of getting sick and taking an antibiotic, only to get sick again, went on for more than five months.

Finally, Phyllis made an appointment to see an ear, nose and throat (ENT) specialist. After conducting a thorough examination and taking detailed X-rays, the ENT concluded that Max kept getting inner ear infections because of a deformity within his ears that prevented them from draining. She said surgery was the only way to correct the problem. Although Phyllis was apprehensive about her baby going under anesthesia and having surgery at such a young age, she and her husband gave their consent and the doctor performed the surgery.

It has been more than a year since Max had the surgery. He has not had one inner ear infection. Phyllis and her husband are elated.

Unlike the pediatrician, who had been treating the symptoms, the ENT got to the cause of the symptoms. Having done that, she was able to recommend the appropriate action to eliminate the inner ear infections once and for all.

We can transfer that approach to the workplace. Suppose you have a 10 percent tardiness rate in your group. Like Max's fever, the tardiness is a symptom of a problem, not the problem itself. If you jump in and begin treating the tardiness, you could find yourself facing the same symptom again and again. As John Foster Dulles said, "The measure of success is not whether you have a tough problem to deal with, but whether it's the same problem you had last year." So, like the ENT, you have to get to what is causing the tardiness.

That is where this book comes in.

Tapping into lessons I have learned during my 20+ years of experience as a Fortune 500 company manager and 10+ years of experience as a consultant to front-line supervisors, I have identified (in no particular order) the 20 most common reasons that employees fail to meet performance expectations.

But I have not stopped there. I have also identified proven solutions that are guaranteed to remove those reasons. Finally, I have included step-by-step instructions on how to implement those solutions. Even if your employees are meeting your performance expectations, the solutions I offer will help you keep their performance at that level, or even raise it to new heights.

All the solutions discussed in this book are based on my belief that employees have unlimited potential for achievement.

I also believe that in order for you to tap into that potential you must:

1. Create a climate that fosters productivity. Bill Hewlett, the founder of Hewlett-Packard had it right when he said, "Men and women want to do a good job, and if you provide them the proper environment, they will do so."

2. Serve your employees, rather than expect them to serve you. As John Maxwell said, "The first step to leadership is servanthood."

3. Avoid operating on any of the following theories:

    a) Employees are tools to be used to accomplish the organization's (or my personal) goals.

    b) My job is to think, their job is to do the work.

    c) Employees cannot be trusted so I have to "ride herd" on them all the time.

4. Be a leader rather than a boss. There are dramatic differences. As Russell Ewing said:

> A boss creates fear; a leader creates confidence.
>
> A boss drives people; a leader guides people.
>
> A boss says, "Do;" a leader says, "Let's do."
>
> A boss relies on authority; a leader relies on cooperation.
>
> A boss fixes blame; a leader corrects mistakes.
>
> A boss knows all; a leader asks questions.
>
> A boss makes work drudgery; a leader makes work interesting.
>
> A boss says "I;" a leader says "We."

Good luck to you as you go about the noble task of serving your employees by helping them perform at their peak capacity.

1

THEY DON'T UNDERSTAND THEIR DUTIES

Don Shula, one of the most successful football coaches of all time, believes that players perform best when they completely understand their duties. That also holds true for employees. However, studies show that 70 percent of American workers do not clearly understand what is expected of them.

Solution: Clearly define employees' duties.

How to implement the solution:

1. Determine their job title.

You may take this directly from the job description (JD). If you have assigned a special job title that is not covered by the JD, update the JD to reflect the new title.

2. Determine the employees' duties.

Develop a statement that contains at least two, but no more than seven, duties for each employee. Consider their skills, the skills they like using most, and the activities that they find most rewarding.

Duty statements usually contain three parts: a verb, an object/person, and a purpose. See Figure 1.1 – Sample Duty Statement for an Office Services Assistant.

3. Establish priorities for employees.

Rank the duties in order of importance, beginning with the most important. Indicate the approximate percentage of time you expect the employee to spend on each duty. You could prioritize as follows:

    a) Prepare travel reports - 60% of the time.

    b) Answer the telephone – 30% of the time.

    c) Direct walk-in applicants – 10% of the time.

See Figure 1.1 – Sample Duty Statement for an Office Services Assistant.

4. Meet one-on-one with employees to:

    a) Review Figure 1.1 – Duty Statement.

    b) Get input on what you have proposed.

    c) Answer any questions they have.

    d) Modify your proposal, if necessary.

    e) Sign the Duty Statement.

    f) Give employees a copy of the Duty Statement.

Figure 1.1

SAMPLE DUTY STATEMENT – OFFICE SERVICES ASSISTANT

Verb	Object/Person	Purpose	Priority
Prepare	Travel reports	Reimbursement	60% of the time
Answer	Telephone	Pre-qualify applicants	30% of the time
Direct	Walk-in applicants	Complete an application	10% of the time

Employee's Signature _____

Date_____

Supervisor's Signature _____

Date_____

ACTION PLAN

Write any ideas you will implement within your work team.

1. _____ .

2. _____ .

3. _____ .

4. _____ .

5. _____ .

2

THEY DON'T KNOW HOW TO PERFORM THEIR DUTIES

Studies show that 50 percent of employees say their organization has not provided adequate training for them to perform their duties.

Solution: Provide appropriate training.

How to implement the solution:

1. Identify the performance deficiency.

2. Determine if it is critical.

   a) If not, take no further action.

   b) If it is:

3. Determine if the deficiency is due to a lack of training by:

   a) Asking the employees.

b) Asking yourself if you have ever seen them perform the duty correctly.

c) Asking yourself if they could perform the duty correctly if their life depended on it.

These questions will help you rule out the possibility that some other factor (a lack of objectives, lack of feedback, personal problems, etc.) is causing the deficiency.

If the performance deficiency is due to a lack of training:

4. Identify various delivery methods, i.e. classroom, self-paced, on-the-job, on-line, etc.

5. Consider:

    a) The cost.

    b) How long it would take.

    c) Demonstrated effectiveness with other employees.

6. Choose a method.

7. Meet with the employees before the training to:

a) Document the current performance on Figure 2.1 - Sample Training Agreement.

b) Document the performance you expect after the training on Figure 2.1 - Sample Training Agreement.

c) Give employees a completed and signed copy of Figure 2.1 - Training Agreement.

d) Explain to your employees how the training will help them accomplish the organizational goals.

e) Explain what they can expect at the training session.

f) Make sure they have any pre-course assignments they need.

g) Identify any obstacles they can expect to encounter as they transfer the new skills to the workplace.

8. Meet with the employees after the training to:

a) Get feedback on what they thought of the training.

b) Provide recognition.

c) Assign them a specific duty related to the recently completed training.

Note: Monitor employees' performance to make sure they can now meet the performance expectations.

Figure 2.1

SAMPLE TRAINING AGREEMENT

Employee: Pauline Smith

Position Title: Customer Service Representative

Date: July 18, 2005

Job Duty: Preparing service orders

Current performance: 85% accuracy rate.

Expected performance after training: 95% accuracy rate.

Employee's Signature _____

Date_____

Supervisor's Signature _____

Date_____

ACTION PLAN

Write any ideas you will implement within your work team.

1._____.

2._____.

3._____.

4._____.

5._____.

3

THEY DON'T UNDERSTAND HOW WELL THEY SHOULD PERFORM THEIR DUTIES

Employees want to do a good job. It would be difficult to find one who gets out of bed in the morning and says, "Well, I am going to go down to the office and see what a poor job I can do today." In addition to wanting to do a good job, they are also *capable* of doing a good job.

However, when their performance falls short of expectations many of them say it is because they do not know how well how they should perform their duties. When asked, "How well are you supposed to perform your job?" they answer with such vague phrases, "I am responsible for providing good customer service." or "My job is to exceed customers' expectations." But they do not know what constitutes "good customer service" or "exceeding customers' expectations".

Solution: Set performance goals.

"If you don't know where you are going you might wind up someplace else."

–Yogi Berra, former baseball player

Studies show that less than 30 percent of supervisors have performance objectives for their employees.

How to implement the solution:

There are two phases of implement: the preparation phase and the implementation phase

Preparation Phase

1. Get the employees involved at the beginning of the evaluation period.

Even though employees want performance objectives, they do not want to have those objectives imposed upon them. Instead, they want to take part in their development. So, while you might develop some preliminary objectives, meet one-on-one with employees to get their input before finalizing them. Hold a team meeting to announce your plans prior to the one-on-one meetings. Everyone will hear the same thing at the same time and they can ask any questions they have. During the team meeting:

a) Tell employees you will meet with them to set objectives.

b) Tell them the areas in which you will set objectives, i.e. sales, customer service, attendance.

c) Give them a copy of Figure 3.1 – Sample Performance Agreement and ask them to list what they think are reasonable objectives in each area.

d) Tell them you will do the same thing.

e) Tell them that when you meet with them you will negotiate and agree on the final objectives.

2. Use the SMARTER method to write a "Draft" of the objectives on Figure 3.1 – Performance Agreement. SMARTER stands for:

❑ Specific.

❑ Measurable.

❑ Agreed to by the employees.

❑ Realistic.

❑ Time definite.

❑ Extra effort.

❑ Related to organization's objectives.

Specific.

The objectives should be specific rather than vague.

Examples of vague objectives:

❑ Do a better job.

❑ Remain on target.

❑ Be a team player.

While these are catchy phrases, they do not tell employees what they are supposed to do.

Examples of specific objectives:

- ❑ Increase sales.

- ❑ Open new territory.

- ❑ Reduce inventory.

Measurable.

This answers the question: "What does success look like?"

Many people laughed at the legislator when he said that, although he could not define pornography, he knew it when he saw it. Unfortunately, some supervisors use a similar approach by telling their employees they don't know what they want but they will know it when they see it. Before you can measure performance you must define what success looks like. It is helpful to consider:

Quantity: How many need to be done? Or how much needs to be done?

Quality: How accurate, thorough or complete should the outcome be?

Examples of measurable success:

- ❑ Increase sales by 25%.

- ❑ Open one new territory.

❏ Reduce inventory by 20%.

Note: Within "Quantity" and "Quality" and it is also helpful to agree on what constitutes:

❏ Fully satisfactory performance.

❏ Outstanding performance.

Agreed to by the employees.

If employees do not agree with the objectives they have no commitment to them, and they may even become "de-motivated." Therefore, it is critical that you get their total buy-in. As Stephen Covey said, "Without buy-in there is no commitment."

Note: It is easier to get that buy-in if you explain how accomplishing the objectives will help employees achieve their personal and professional objectives.

Realistic.

Although objectives should be ambitious, employees must feel that they have a reasonable chance of achieving them. If not, they simply will not put forth much effort. To make objectives realistic, consider the employees':

❏ Experience.

❏ Training.

❏ Previous results.

❏ Demonstrated capabilities.

Time definite.

You and the employees should agree on a specific time frame in which they will meet the objectives.

Examples:

- ❏ Increase sales by 25% by the 1st quarter, 2005.

- ❏ Open 1 new territory by the end of June 2006.

- ❏ Reduce inventory by 20% by December 2007.

- ❏ Achieve 98% customer satisfaction by July 2006.

Extra effort.

The objectives should challenge them to stretch. As former General Electric CEO Jack Welch said, "You should instill in your employees the idea that they should go beyond ordinary objectives."

Related to the organization's objectives.

The more people understand the value of what they are doing, the more motivated they are to do well.

–Dr. David Campbell, psychologist

Studies show that 74 percent of employees do not understand their organization's mission and objectives or how their performance impacts them. Help your employees understand by answering three important questions:

1) What is your organization's mission?

As an example, the federal Office of Personnel Management's (OPM) mission is:

a) To effectively recruit, develop, manage, and retain a high quality and diverse workforce even as the labor market and the workplace undergo significant and continuous change.

b) To consistently honor merit principles in managing its workforce.

c) To provide high quality, cost-effective human resources services to meet the evolving needs of federal agencies, employees, retirees, their families, and the public.

d) To safeguard the employee benefit trust funds with financial excellence and integrity.

2) What are your organization's goals?

As an example, OPM's objectives are:

a) To reduce the time needed to process Federal Employees Retirement System (FERS) claims to an average of 90 days.

b) To reduce claims processing error rates by 10 percent.

c) To have 80 percent of the customers receive their check before it is expected.

d) To achieve a 95 percent customer satisfaction level.

3) What products or services does your work unit provide that can help the organization reach its objectives?

As an example, suppose you are the OPM mailroom supervisor. You can see how getting the checks sorted and delivered to the post office promptly can help the organization reach its objective of having 80 percent of the customers receive their check before it is expected.

Note: If your work unit generates a product or service that does not affect the organization's objectives, you should analyze the situation. You may want to eliminate that product or service.

A man saw two workers breaking granite and stopped to talk. He asked one worker, "What are you doing?" The worker replied, "I'm trying to break this granite."

He said to the second man, "What are you doing?" The man said, "I am part of a team that is building a great cathedral."

The second worker could see the big picture and how his tasks fit into the organizational objectives.

3. Determine how you will monitor employees' performance.

Failure to do so means you will not have any tangible evidence to support feedback that you give. Some ways to accomplish this are:

a) Direct observation.

b) Audits of time logs/work reports.

c) Customer compliments/complaints.

d) Feedback from coworkers, peers, other supervisors, or customers.

Get a representative picture of their overall work. The best approach is to sample the work in many different circumstances; i.e. on a typical day, on a busy day; for complex projects and for routine ones; sometimes in the morning, sometimes in the afternoon.

Incidentally, an added benefit of having performance objectives is that employees can monitor their performance and make adjustments without you having to say anything. Of course they will need access to results in order to do this.

4. Determine how you will document the results of your monitoring.

This will give you written information to which you can refer when you give feedback, whether informally or during the final performance evaluation process. One method is a Performance Log - Figure 3.2. In order for it to work effectively:

a) Make entries weekly throughout the evaluation period so you don't lose track of critical information.

b) Record factual data, not subjective things like "attitude."

c) Include both positive and negative things.

d) Purge outdated information so it does not color your thinking about current performance.

5. Determine the frequency and type of performance feedback you will give.

It is a good idea to give formal, written feedback at predetermined intervals, i.e. monthly, quarterly, and semi-annually. You can give informal verbal feedback even more frequently.

6. Determine the rewards for meeting goals and the penalties for not meeting them.

In the movie Remember the Titans, T.C. Williams High School had just been integrated. The new football coach, Herman Boone (played by Denzel Washington), was trying to get his players to cross racial lines, get to know each other, and build team spirit. Despite his attempts, the two groups would not even talk to each other. At training camp meals, for example, the Caucasian players ate together and the Black players ate together.

Finally, Coach Boone had had enough. He told his players that if they ignored each other they would keep on having two daily practices in the stifling August heat and humidity. If they still ignored each other they would go to three practices per day, followed by four practices. The reward, on the other hand, would be one shorter practice session per day.

So the players knew the rewards and the penalties.

Implementation Phase

This refers to the one-on-one meetings with the employees. During these meetings:

1. Negotiate what each employee must do in order to achieve a Fully Satisfactory Performance Rating and an Outstanding Performance Rating. (Record this on Figure 3.1-Performance Agreement.)

2. Agree on how you will monitor employee performance.

3. Agree on how you will document the results of your monitoring. (See Figure 3.2 - Performance Log)

4. Agree on the frequency and type of performance feedback you will give.

5. Agree on the rewards (more autonomy, more responsibility, a more flexible schedule, material awards such as dinners or trips, increased visibility or a promotion) for accomplishing the goals and the penalties for not accomplishing them.

6. Make it clear that you are there to provide support as needed and that you will hold at least four status meetings with the employees.

Status Meeting #1 (See Figure 3.3)

To be held within a month of the beginning of the evaluation period. During this meeting:

- ❑ Review the objectives and the status.
- ❑ Identify any start-up problems.
- ❑ Determine if the objectives are realistic.
- ❑ Determine if the time frames are realistic.
- ❑ Establish a date for the second status meeting.

Status Meeting #2 (See Figure 3.4)

To be held approximately three months into the evaluation period. During this meeting:

- ❑ Review the objectives and the status.
- ❑ Determine if the work is on schedule.
- ❑ Identify any new issues that have come up.
- ❑ Establish a date for the third status meeting.

Status Meeting #3 (See Figure 3.5)

To be held approximately nine months into the evaluation period. During this meeting:

- ❑ Review the objectives and the status.
- ❑ Identify any last-minute changes.
- ❑ Establish the date for the final status meeting.

Final Status Meeting #4 (See Figure 3.6)

To be held the end of the evaluation period. During this meeting compare the results with the objectives.

7. Sign and give employees a copy of Figure 3.1 – Performance Agreement.

Figure 3.1

SAMPLE PERFORMANCE AGREEMENT

Employee: Joseph Brown

Job Title: Human Resources Assistant, GS-0203

Date Prepared: April 19, 2005

Job Duty #1: Provide customer service

To achieve a fully satisfactory rating, the employee must meet all of the following requirements:

1. Respond to each customer request with accurate and complete information.

2. Respond to Email requests within 5 workdays of receipt of the request.

3. Respond to formal written correspondence within 10 workdays of receipt of the request.

4. Mail the requested information within 3 workdays of receipt of the request.

5. If requested material is unavailable, notify the customers when they can expect to receive it.

6. Accomplish this by the end of the evaluation period.

Figure 3.1 Page 2

SAMPLE PERFORMANCE AGREEMENT

To achieve an outstanding rating, the employee must meet all of the fully satisfactory standards PLUS:

1. Receive at least three written commendations from customers.

2. On their initiative, assume and accomplish a minimum of three customer satisfaction tasks that go beyond the assigned duties.

3. Proactively communicate with a minimum of three customers per week to assess their needs.

4. Accomplish this by the end of the evaluation period.

Note: Performance that falls below fully satisfactory is rated less than satisfactory.

Employee's Signature _____

Date_____

Supervisor's Signature _____

Date_____

Figure 3.2

PERFORMANCE LOG

Employee _____

Position Title _____

When (Date the event occurred):

What (Write a brief description of the event):

Where (Indicate where the event occurred):

Why (Describe why it either meets or fails to meet expectations):

Source of information (Direct observation, customer comment, other supervisor comment, production report etc.):

Mitigating circumstances (Explanation of factors that may have impacted the employee's ability to meet performance expectations, i.e. illness, a change in duty assignment, implementation of a new procedure, etc.):

WHY EMPLOYEES FAIL TO MEET PERFORMANCE EXPECTATIONS

Figure 3.3

STATUS MEETING #1

Employee _____

Position Title _____

Date _____

| Job Duty #1 | Objective | Status |

| Job Duty #2 | Objective | Status |

| Job Duty #3 | Objective | Status |

Date of next status meeting _____

Employee's Signature _____

Supervisor's Signature _____

Figure 3.4

STATUS MEETING #2

Employee _____

Position Title _____

Date _____

Job Duty #1   Objective   Status

Job Duty #2   Objective   Status

Job Duty #3   Objective   Status

Date of next status meeting _____

Employee's Signature _____

Supervisor's Signature _____

Figure 3.5

STATUS MEETING #3

Employee _____

Position Title _____

Date _____

Job Duty #1   Objective   Status

Job Duty #2   Objective   Status

Job Duty #3   Objective   Status

Date of next status meeting _____

Employee's Signature _____

Supervisor's Signature _____

Figure 3.6

FINAL STATUS MEETING

Employee _____

Position Title _____

Date _____

Job Duty #1	Objective	Status
Job Duty #2	Objective	Status
Job Duty #3	Objective	Status

Employee's Signature_____

Supervisor's Signature _____

ACTION PLAN

Write any ideas you will implement within your work team.

1._____.

2._____.

3._____.

4._____.

5. _____.

Why employees fail to meet performance expectations

4

THEIR SKILLS DO NOT MATCH THE POSITION REQUIREMENTS

The second fundamental belief held by Coach Don Shula is that players perform at their highest level when their skills match the requirements of the role the coach asks them to play. The same is true of employees.

Solution: Match each employee's skills to the position requirements.

How to implement the solution:

1. Think about the employees' position.

2. On Figure 4.1 – Skills Worksheet, list the skills the position requires. Some examples are:

- ❑ Oral communication

- ❑ Problem-solving

- ❑ Creativity

- Flexibility

- Aggressiveness

- Enthusiasm

3. On a scale of 0 to 10 with 0 not being critical at all and 10 being very critical, assign a number to each skill to indicate how important it is in performing the duties of the position.

- Oral communication

- Problem-solving

- Creativity

- Flexibility

- Aggressiveness

- Enthusiasm

4. On a scale of 0 to 10 with 0 indicating that the employees do not possess this skill at all to 10 indicating that they possess it in abundance, indicate how much of the skill they possess.

- Oral communication

- Problem-solving

- Creativity

- Flexibility

□ Aggressiveness

□ Enthusiasm

If the position requires a great deal of creativity (say, "10") and in your view the employee possesses a low amount of creativity (say, "2"), then as they say, "Houston, we have a problem."

In that case, you may want to either reassign the employees to a position with requirements that more closely match his or her abilities, or change the requirements of his or her current position to match his or her abilities.

5. Another helpful tool in matching employees' abilities to a position is a Personality Inventory. (Figure 4.2 – Personality Types) With this inventory you can:

a) Identify the personality type that you think best matches each employee.

b) Ask employees to identify the personality type they think best matches them.

c) Assign duties that best match the agreed-upon personality type. (Use Figure 4.3)

Figure 4.1

Skills Worksheet

Skills Required	How critical are skills (0 – 10)	Amount of skill the employee possesses (0 – 10)

Figure 4.2

PERSONALITY TYPES

1. The Technocrat.

   ❏ Driven by the desire to excel.

   ❏ Likes to continue to build skills.

   ❏ Likes to be known as an expert.

   When assigning job duties:

   ❏ Allow them to use their technical skills.

   ❏ Allow them to develop new technical skills.

   ❏ Allow them to specialize in a particular skill area.

2. The Yuppie.

   ❏ Likes promotions/money.

   ❏ Likes to learn skills to climb the career ladder.

   ❏ Likes to gain increasing authority.

   When assigning job duties:

   ❏ Allow them to develop a wide range of skills.

   ❏ Give them an opportunity to make decisions.

   ❏ Provide visibility that could lead to a promotion.

Figure 4.2 Page 2

PERSONALITY TYPES

3. The Lone Ranger.

- ❑ Freedom is a key driving force.

- ❑ Does not like a lot of rules.

When assigning duties:

- ❑ Tell them what you want and get out of the way.

- ❑ Allow them to work according to their own rules.

4. Mr./Ms. Security/Stability.

- ❑ Likes things to be routine and predictable.

- ❑ Likes clearly defined policies and procedures.

When assigning duties:

- ❑ Tell them what to do and how to do it.

- ❑ Assign duties that are repetitive in nature.

- ❑ Keep change to a minimum.

Figure 4.2 Page 3

PERSONALITY TYPES

5. The Entrepreneur.

   ❑ Becomes bored with routine.

   ❑ Likes to develop new ways of doing things.

   When assigning duties:

   ❑ Assign new projects.

   ❑ Allow them to be creative.

6. The Advocate.

   ❑ Money and promotion are not terribly important.

   ❑ Likes to make a difference in people's lives.

   When assigning duties:

   ❑ Include tasks that impact lives, i.e. processing benefit claims.

7. The Challenge Seeker.

   ❑ Easily bored with routine.

   ❑ Likes tough challenges.

   When assigning duties:

   ❑ Allow them to compete against others.

   ❑ Set high expectations.

   ❑ Assign one challenging project after another.

Figure 4.2 Page 4

PERSONALITY TYPES

8. The Family Man/Woman.

   ❏ Family oriented.

   ❏ Works to live, rather than the other way around.

   When assigning duties:

   ❏ Show how duties can help them meet family needs.

   ❏ Focus on getting job done, not necessarily working a set number of hours.

   ❏ Allow a daily flexible schedule, if possible.

   ❏ Allow them to telecommute at least one day per week.

Figure 4.3

DUTY ASSIGNMENT WORKSHEET

Employee _____

Position Title _____

Date _____

Duties: _____

_____

Employee's Signature _____

Supervisor's Signature _____

ACTION PLAN

Write any ideas you will implement within your work team.

1 _____.

2 _____.

3 _____.

4 _____.

5 _____.

5

THEY DON'T KNOW THEY ARE NOT MEETING EXPECTATIONS

The date was October 25, 1964. The Minnesota Vikings were playing the San Francisco 49ers at Kezar Stadium in San Francisco. Jim Marshall, an extremely conscientious player who never missed a game, was playing right defensive end for the Vikings. Early in the game there was a fumble. Spotting the ball laying on the ground, Jim immediately picked it up. As soon as he did he became entangled with other players and he was spun around a couple of times. Finally, he was in the clear with nothing but green grass in front of him. His arms and legs pumped as he gained speed. Soon Jim was running as fast as he could. In a very short time he arrived in the end zone - 66 yards from the spot he had picked up the fumbled football. He was elated and was about to celebrate having scored a touchdown. Then it dawned on him-he had run 66 yards in the wrong direction. His goal had been to do a good job (score a touchdown) for his team; instead he had scored a safety for San Francisco.

That incident reminds me of some employees.

Like Jim, they show up every day.

Like Jim, they want to do a good job and help their team win.

Like Jim, they think they are doing a good job when, in fact, they are going in the wrong direction.

Like Jim, by the time they find out they are going in the wrong direction, it is too late to do anything about it.

Solution: Provide corrective feedback.

As management guru Ken Blanchard says, "Feedback is the breakfast of champions."

If Jim Marshall had known he was headed in the wrong direction before he got to the end zone he could have reversed his field and headed in the right direction. Likewise, if your employees know they are headed in the wrong direction before the end of the evaluation period, they, too, can reverse their field and improve their performance.

Despite its importance, studies show that 60 percent of employees say their supervisor does not give them regular performance feedback. Some say they only get it at the end of the year. "I thought I was doing what my supervisor expected of me" is a comment I often hear from employees after they receive their annual performance appraisal. Others say they do not get any feedback at all. "I don't know how I am doing" is a comment I hear from them.

How to implement the solution:

1. **Recognize that your goals are to:**

   a) Change the employee's behavior.

   b) Not damage the relationship.

2. Give feedback regularly.

For maximum effectiveness, feedback should be ongoing. Think about school. Instead of waiting until the end of the school year to give feedback, most teachers give quizzes, a mid term and a final examination. At any point, students can tell how they are doing. Likewise, employees should be able to tell how they are doing at any point during the evaluation period.

3. Review your documentation prior to meeting with the employees.

Since this prepares you to support your comments with examples, review your notes and any other supporting information, i.e. production reports, incident reports, letters or comments that you have received, etc.

4. Give feedback in private.

The setting is very important. Arrange for an environment in which you will not be overheard or interrupted.

5. Make it clear that your purpose is to assist the employee in achieving personal and professional success.

You are not out to punish or embarrass them.

6. Pick an appropriate time.

Avoid giving feedback if you are angry, such as after a major performance failure. You could say things that might cause additional performance woes.

7. Avoid drawing a conclusion about why the employee is not meeting expectations.

"The problem with you, Michael, is that you are careless," is an example of drawing a conclusion. Instead, allow employees to explain. Perhaps they lack the necessary skills, or maybe there are other factors that are preventing them from achieving the objectives.

8. Never yell or threaten employees.

Avoid comments like, "Tommy, if you don't improve your performance you are going to be fired!!"

9. Avoid trapping the employees.

"How many times have I told you to fax a copy of the report to the billing office?" If you are like me you hated it when your parents asked you that question. Employees also hate it.

10. Begin with appreciation.

A barber always lathers up a person before a shave. So don't forget to tell them what they are doing well.

11. Be specific.

Describe the undesirable performance in exact terms, i.e. "50% percent of the invoices contained at least one error."

12. Reach agreement on the specific problem.

If you say 50% of the invoices had errors and the employee says the error rate was half that, you must resolve that discrepancy before you can proceed.

13. Assume some of the blame.

This helps prevent defensiveness. You might say something like, "I should have done a better job of explaining why this was important."

14. Describe the specific results you want and why.

"We need you to achieve a 98% customer satisfaction level. Our funding will be reduced if we fail."

15. Relate accomplishing what you want to something they want.

"You know, Shelly, meeting this objective will enable you to develop the added qualifications you need in order to apply for the position of Senior Analyst."

16. Make the problem seem easy to fix.

John Robinson, former coach of the Los Angeles Rams, said, "If a player made a mistake I reminded him that he was nearly perfect, but now was a good time to work on the one thing left." You might say, "The only thing you have to do is to check the results one final time before you submit the report."

17. Assure them they can do what you are asking.

You could say, "I am confident that you can turn this around during the next quarter."

18. Brainstorm with employees to identify alternative ways to improve performance.

They will be less likely to resist the improvement steps if they are involved in their development. So let them generate some ideas. You could say something like, "I have some thoughts, but first I would like to hear what you think would help you improve your performance."

19. Develop a Performance Improvement Plan.

Use the ideas from the brainstorming session to formulate a Performance Improvement Plan. (See Figure 5.1).

Figure 5.1

PERFORMANCE IMPROVEMENT PLAN

Employee _____

Position _____

Date _____

Performance deficiency (Please place a √ in the appropriate area):

___ Attendance/Tardiness ___ Quality___ Quantity

___ Other (please specify)

_____

Indicate:

The current performance in objective terms, i.e. completing 10 cases per month.

The expected performance in objective terms, i.e. completing 15 cases per month.

The specific action the employee will take to move from the current performance to the expected performance.

The date the employee will have achieved the desired performance.

Employee's Signature & Date _____

Supervisor's Signature & Date _____

ACTION PLAN

Write any ideas you will implement within your work team.

1. _____.

2. _____.

3. _____.

4. _____.

5. _____.

6

THEY RECEIVE NO RECOGNITION FOR MEETING EXPECTATIONS

Employees consistently say the number one thing they want from their supervisors is recognition for a job well done. Studies show that 88 percent of employees say they do not receive enough, even though recognition can be simple and inexpensive. Their bosses apparently operate on the notion, "This is a test. It is only a test. Had it been a real job you would have received recognition, promotions and raises."

Solution: Provide appropriate recognition.

"I can live for two months on a good compliment."

- Mark Twain, humorist

How to implement the solution:

1. Set individual performance objectives.

Many times employees are turned off because they believe recognition programs are designed for only the "favorites" to receive awards.

Performance objectives can eliminate this concern since they provide an impartial way of selecting employees to be recognized.

They may be based on percent improvement, total sales revenue, customer satisfaction, etc. (Review Cause #3).

2. Base recognition on achievement of objectives.

This is the second step in eliminating the appearance of playing favorites.

3. Identify the appropriate recognition for each employee.

Sometimes supervisors incorrectly assume that the recognition that motivates them will have the same impact on their employees. Let me give you an example.

Even though he had only been a supervisor for a short time Melvin had become very frustrated and discouraged. His team was responsible for processing benefit claims. The objective was to render a decision to each customer within five workdays of receiving the claim. Melvin's employees were typically taking 10 to 15 workdays (or longer) to render a decision.

Before he had been promoted, Melvin had been the most productive person on another team that had the same responsibility as the team he now managed. In fact he usually rendered a decision within two workdays of receiving the claim. His proficiency had helped him get promoted to his current position.

Since Melvin had been motivated by the challenge of achieving lofty objectives, he assumed that his employees would be too. He kept telling them "When I had your job...." However, that did nothing to improve their productivity.

This was the point at which I met Melvin.

After listening to his story, I told Melvin that all employees are motivated by What's In It For Me (WIIFM). I went on to tell him that WIIFM varies from one employee to another, and his employees' WIIFM was probably different from his. His challenge was to find each employee's WIIFM and meet it.

To illustrate my point I told Melvin about my 12-year old nephew who recently visited from Brooklyn, New York. During his weekend visit I had a lot of yard work to do (mowing, edging and trimming bushes). I got him to spend about three hours helping me. Now did he suddenly get excited about doing yard work? Not really. Then how did I get him to agree to spend three hours on a hot Saturday afternoon doing work that he detests? I told him that after we finished we would go to his favorite restaurant (Red Lobster) and he could order anything on the menu. So you can say I "motivated" him by appealing to his WIIFM. I went on to point out that, while going to Red Lobster was not my WIIFM, it worked for my nephew. Since he was the person I was trying to motivate, I went with **his** WIIFM, not mine.

Employees, like my nephew, are motivated by their own WIIFM. I suggested to Melvin that he:

a) Review the Figure 6.1 Personality Types and identify the personality type that he thinks best describes each of his employees.

b) Give each employee a copy of Personality Types -Figure 6.1 and ask employees to identify the personality type they think best describes them.

c) Meet one-on-one with employees to compare his perceptions to theirs. Agree on the personality type.

d) Review Figure 6.2 – Ideas for Recognition.

e) Give recognition that meets their WIIFM.

When I met with Melvin six months later he told me he had followed the steps I had recommended. He was simply amazed at the improvement in his employees' productivity.

4. Make recognition timely.

As management expert Steven Kerr said, "If a rat in a cage pulls a lever and nine months later you give him a cube of sugar, he is not likely to connect the reward to pulling a lever." Likewise, in order for employees to connect the recognition to a specific achievement, make sure you award it immediately after that achievement. In fact, one of the most effective ways is to catch them doing exactly what you want and to give them a verbal "high five" right then.

After all, the five most important words in the English language are, "You did a great job."

As Fred Bucy, past president of Texas Instruments said, "It doesn't take much talent to issue orders. But it takes continued discipline to study the variety of people you are leading in order to understand what it takes to motivate them to do their best to make the company and themselves a success."

Figure 6.1

PERSONALITY TYPES

1. The Technocrat.

   ❏ Money/promotions are not driving forces.

   ❏ Likes to continue to build skills.

   Best ways to recognize:

   ❏ Allow them to attend a special course or conference in which they can continue to build new skills.

2. The Yuppie.

   ❏ Likes promotions/money.

   ❏ Likes to do many things.

   ❏ Likes to get information from several sources and to organize it.

   ❏ Eager to learn new things that can help them move up and gain additional authority.

   Best ways to recognize:

   ❏ More money.

   ❏ A high visibility project.

   ❏ A prestigious job title.

   ❏ A promotion.

Figure 6.1 - Page 2

PERSONALITY TYPES

3. The Lone Ranger.

   ❑ Likes to know what you want and to be left alone to figure out how to do it.

   ❑ Does not like rules.

   ❑ Is not overly concerned with promotion/prestige.

   Best ways to recognize:

   ❑ Let them do their "Own thing".

4. Mr./Ms. Security/Stability.

   ❑ Likes to know (often) how they are doing.

   ❑ Likes to know what is going on in the organization.

   Best ways to recognize:

   ❑ Take them out to lunch.

   ❑ Let them know what is going on in the organization.

   ❑ Follow up regularly to offer encouragement.

Figure 6.1 - Page 3

PERSONALITY TYPES

5. The Entrepreneur.

   ❑ Likes to generate new ideas and ways of doing things.

   Best ways to recognize:

   ❑ Allow them to design a new work process or lead a project.

6. The Advocate.

   ❑ Very idealistic.

   ❑ Has strong ideas on how the world should be.

   ❑ Likes to connect the dots between work and their beliefs about how the world should be.

   Best ways to recognize:

   ❑ Allow them to use their talents improve others' conditions, i.e. working with company-sponsored community programs, helping customers get the benefits they deserve, helping women or minorities achieve their career goals, etc.

Figure 6.1 - Page 4

PERSONALITY TYPES

7. The Challenger Seeker.

   ❑ Lives for a challenge.

   ❑ Is excited by high goals.

   Best ways to recognize:

   ❑ Allow them to work on challenging projects.

   ❑ Assign challenging assignments in succession.

8. The Family Man/Woman.

   ❑ Family oriented.

   ❑ Focus on getting job done, not necessarily working a set number of hours.

   Best ways to recognize:

   ❑ Time off to spend with family. One idea is to give them a two-hour lunch.

   ❑ Family events such as planning company picnics.

These are general guidelines. Make sure you ask employees what kinds of recognition would motivate them.

Figure 6.2 Page 1

40 IDEAS FOR RECOGNITION

Here are some additional ways you might provide acknowledgement for a job well done:

1. Encourage peer recognition.

Recognition by one's peers can be even more motivating than recognition by supervisors. Employees know who works hard and deserves recognition. One of the reasons being named Coach of the Year in professional football means so much is because the 28 head coaches determine the winner, not sportswriters or fans. Using the idea of peer recognition, one company initiated a "Caught in the Act Program", encouraging employees to write up a co-worker who has done a good job in any performance area.

2. Send flowers.

3. Mail a personal thank-you note to employees' home.

4. Get a senior executive to say "thanks" for a job well done.

They can do this face-to-face, with a memo or even a voice message.

Figure 6.2 Page 2

40 IDEAS FOR RECOGNITION

5. Give employees their own business cards.

People like to feel important. Having business cards showing their title goes a long way towards accomplishing that.

6. Have a restaurant cater lunch.

7. Post customer appreciation letters on a bulletin board.

The letters can be from internal as well as external customers. Post a picture of the employee next to the letter.

8. Serve pizza.

9. Select an employee of the month.

Phoenix Textiles goes so far as to allow the employee of the month to park near the front entrance right next to the company president's space.

10. Summon employees to your office just to give them a pat on the back.

Once they are there, simply thank them for their good work or special effort. Having done that, dismiss them without talking about any other business matters.

Figure 6.2 Page 3

40 IDEAS FOR RECOGNITION

11. Do their least desirable task for an hour.

12. Display photos of outstanding achievers.

13. Pass on positive comments.

When you hear a positive remark, repeat it to that person as soon as possible. Seek them out, if necessary. As management expert Robert Henry said, "A man doesn't live by bread alone. He needs buttering up once in a while."

14. Allow top performers to spearhead a new project.

15. Provide variety to their duties.

16. Allow them to learn a new technology.

17. Give them more autonomy.

If my service representatives did not have any errors on their service orders for six months in a row, they got to bypass the review process and input their orders directly into the billing system. They felt trusted and almost all of them aspired to achieve this privilege.

Figure 6.2 Page 4

40 IDEAS FOR RECOGNITION

18. Give employees more responsibility.

As an example, once employees demonstrate a certain level of proficiency, allow them to train other employees on their methods.

19. Allow them to showcase their skills.

As an example, let them give a presentation to upper management or to another manager's group.

20. Allow them to attend a special class or conference.

21. Serve them a meal.

As an expression of gratitude, put on a chef's hat and apron and serve them breakfast or lunch.

22. Provide a dinner gift certificate for two.

23. Name an award after a top performer.

Since Dick Butkus was the epitome of what a linebacker should be, each year the outstanding linebacker in college football receives the Dick Butkus Award. Borrow that idea and name an award after an employee who consistently demonstrates the qualities you would like your entire team to exhibit.

Figure 6.2 Page 5

40 IDEAS FOR RECOGNITION

24. Read customer thank you letters in team meetings.

25. Invite employees to have lunch with you.

26. Distribute poker chips for outstanding contributions.

Allow them to redeem the chips for a special prize.

27. Award a gift certificate for a massage.

28. Give away tickets to movies or local sporting events.

29. Meet with employees one-on-one.

They will love to have you listen (really listen) to their thoughts, ideas and issues.

30. Establish a special job title.

As a service representative, Barbara was responsible for taking orders for new service, arranging to move service from one location to another and contacting customers whose bills were about to fall into delinquent status. Most of the representatives hated calling these customers.

Figure 6.2 Page 6

40 IDEAS FOR RECOGNITION

However, Barbara not only loved doing it but she was very good at it. So, I appointed her the office "Collections Specialist". This was a win-win-win situation. Barbara won because she got to do something at which she excelled, the other representatives won because they no longer had to do this unpleasant task, and I won because, since Barbara did such a superb job, the amount of money we had to write off each month as uncollectible dropped by 15%.

31. Give them a hot air balloon ride.

32. Give an extra hour off for lunch.

33. Award a get away weekend.

34. Pay for babysitting for a night out.

35. Give time off for completing a project ahead of schedule.

36. Allow employees to work a daily flexible schedule.

37. Allow them to telecommute one day per week.

Figure 6.2 Page 7

40 IDEAS FOR RECOGNITION

38. Allow them to select the duties they like to perform most.

39. Send birthday and anniversary of employment cards signed by a top executive.

40. Give a certificate for a free housecleaning.

As you can see, there is no limit to the possibilities. It does not matter how ridiculous it seems to you. The important thing is that the employees appreciate it. One supervisor I know, Chuck, used to hand out gold stars to his employees who had met certain criteria for the week. Other supervisors thought it was a dumb idea at first. But the employees loved it, and they looked forward to Friday to see who would get one of Chuck's gold stars.

So, whatever means you decide to use, give recognition. As management consultant, Thomas J. Frye so eloquently put it, "People work harder and smarter if they find their work satisfactory and know it is appreciated."

Caveats:

1. Ask employees how they would like to receive the recognition. Some people are embarrassed when they are complimented in front of others.

2. For those employees it might be best to point out their achievements in one-on-one meetings. Others

like to be acknowledged in public. Make their recognition more visible.

3. Although it is good to praise employees, you should not overdo it, lest they doubt your sincerity.

I think you will enjoy the poem "If I were Boss:"

If I Were Boss
−Anonymous

If I were boss I would like to say:
"You did a good job here today."
I would look for a man, or girl or boy
Whose heart would leap with a thrill of joy?
At a word of praise, and I'd pass it out
Where the crowd could hear as I walked about.
If I were boss I would like to find
The fellow whose work is the proper kind;
And whenever to me a good thing came
I'd like to be told the toiler's name,
And I'd go to him, and I'd pat his back,
And I'd say, "That was perfectly splendid, Jack!"

Now a bit of praise isn't much to give
But it's dear to the hearts of all that live;
And there's never a man on this good old earth
Who isn't glad to be told he's been of worth;
And a kindly word, when the work is fair,
Is welcome and wanted everywhere.

If I were boss I'm sure I would
Say a kindly word whenever I could.
For a man who has given his best by day

Wants a little more than his weekly pay;
He likes to know with the setting sun,
That the boss is pleased with the work he's done.

ACTION PLAN

Write any ideas you will implement within your work team.

1. _____.

2. _____.

3. _____.

4. _____.

5. _____.

7

THERE ARE BARRIERS IN THE WORK PROCESS

Cheryl had recently been appointed Billing Supervisor for a medical supply company. From her orientation with the Operations Manager she had learned that:

1. The billing clerks were invoicing the insurance companies an average of 81 days after the supplies had gone out.

2. The company was receiving payment approximately 91 days after supplies had gone out.

3. Accounts receivables averaged $300,000 per month.

4. The company was having cash flow problems.

5. The Operation's Manager was convinced that the late payments were due to the lackadaisical attitude of the billing clerks. His thinking was, "If only we had the right people, this would not be happening."

6. Cheryl's mandate was to speed up the payment process.

When employees fail to meet performance expectations, the Operations Manager had done what supervisors sometimes do - blame the employees (in this case-the billing clerks).

However, the primary cause of the failure is often the work process, not the people working within the process. In fact, according to some quality management gurus, 85 percent of the problems organizations face is process related, and only 15 percent are people related.

Solution: Remove the barriers.

How to implement the solution:

1. Examine the inputs into your group.

a) What is the source of information?

When Cheryl did her analysis of the shipping and billing processes, she learned that the shipping clerks manually prepared a packing slip, put a copy into the box and shipped it along with the medical supplies. They also faxed a copy to the billing office.

b) Is the information complete?

Cheryl found that the packing slip was all that the billing clerks needed in order to prepare an invoice.

c) Is the information accurate?

The packing slips were accurate.

d) Is the information on time?

Cheryl discovered the cause of the delay in issuing an invoice. Since the shipping clerks did not know that the billing clerks relied on the packing slip to tell them they should render an invoice, faxing over a copy of the packing slip was a low priority. In fact, they only faxed it over when they got around to it or when their supervisor reminded

them - an average of 79 days after the supplies had
been shipped.

2. Examine the internal work process.

a) Do employees know all the steps to follow?

Cheryl's employees knew all the steps to follow in
order to render an invoice.

b) What obstacles do they encounter? i.e. having
to wait in line to make copies, having to share a
computer, etc.)

Cheryl did not discover any obstacles in the internal
work process.

3. Examine the outputs.

a) Do employees understand the finished product
they are expected to deliver?

The billing clerks understood that the finished product
was an invoice.

b) Do they know to whom they are to deliver the
finished product and in what format?

The billing clerks knew that they needed to send the
invoice to the insurance companies, and they were
following the prescribed format.

c) Do they know when they are expected to deliver
the finished product?

The billing clerks were sending out an invoice within
an average of two days after they received a copy of
the packing slip. So even though they were giving an

"A" Plus effort the net effect was a "C" Minus result as far as the company cash flow was concerned.

4. Establish procedures that help prevent delays and mistakes.

After she completed her analysis Cheryl met with the shipping supervisor and told him what she had discovered. They decided to put together a process improvement team comprised of employees from the billing and the shipping departments. Their task was to develop a way to get the packing slip from the shipping department to the billing department faster. Working with the Information Technology Staff, they mechanized the preparation and distribution of the packing slip. Now, when the shipping clerks prepare a packing slip, the system automatically generates a copy to go into the box with the supplies and distributes a copy to the billing office. Each morning, Cheryl prints copies of the packing slips and assigns them to the appropriate billing clerk. (She has assigned each billing clerk responsibility for handling specific zip codes.) Once the clerks receive the copy of the packing slips, they prepare an invoice and mail it to the insurance companies, usually the same day, but always within two business days.

With a click of the mouse, Cheryl can monitor the entire workflow and take immediate corrective action, if necessary.

Now, the company is receiving payment from the insurance companies within an average of 15 days (instead of 91 days) after shipping the supplies. Needless to say, the Operations Manager considers Cheryl an outstanding supervisor.

ACTION PLAN

Write any ideas you will implement within your work team.

1._____.

2._____.

3._____.

4._____.

5._____.

WHY EMPLOYEES FAIL TO MEET PERFORMANCE EXPECTATIONS

8

THE EXPECTATIONS ARE IMPOSSIBLE TO ACHIEVE

According to social scientists, employees have a high need to achieve. However, they must perceive that they have a realistic chance of achieving in order for them to put forth effort. That means that if your employees believe the expectations that you set are impossible to achieve, they will not even try to achieve them. Some examples of impossible expectations:

1. Achieving 100% increase in sales when customers are cutting their spending.

2. Never receiving a customer complaint.

3. Never fumbling a football.

Solution: Set goals high, but not so high as to be impossible to achieve.

How to implement the solution:

Read Chapter #3 – Performance objectives.

ACTION PLAN

Write any ideas you will implement within your work team.

1._____.

2._____.

3._____.

4._____.

5._____.

9

THEY ARE NOT COMMITTED TO THE WORK PROCESS

As the maintenance supervisor for a food processing plant, Mike was responsible for keeping the machines working to power the production lines. He was the "Don't ask me any questions/just do what I tell you" type. Like so many supervisors, he overlooked the possibility that his employees may be an untapped gold mine of good ideas. Sometimes supervisors do this because they think they have exclusive domain on good ideas. In other cases they may feel threatened by subordinates who are highly creative. Whatever Mike's reasons, he did not seek input from his employees. As a result, they were not committed to the work process, or to achieving the results that he wanted. Consequently, even though he had experienced technicians working for him, Mike was struggling to keep the production lines running 75% of the time, let alone the 90% that the general manager wanted.

Solution: Involve employees in making decisions and solving problems.

As Stephen Covey said, "Without involvement, there is no commitment."

Since being "in on things" empowers employees, they say this is one of the main things they want from their supervisors. Yet, 60 percent of employees say their supervisor does not seek their input when making decisions that affect them. Hence, they may have a low commitment to the work process.

How to implement the solution:

1. Practice participative management.

As consultant Mary Poole said, "Leadership should be more participative than directive."

Let us say there is an issue to be resolved. I told Mike he could use:

Level 1: Make a decision and announce it to the team.

- ❏ Advantage: It is fast.

- ❏ Disadvantage: Workers may not be committed to making it happen.

Level 2: Make a tentative decision and present it, but tell employees he is open to their input, and based on their input he could change his mind.

- ❏ Advantage: Employees can influence the decision.

- ❏ Disadvantage: They may think he is not serious about wanting input.

Level 3: Present the issue, ask for ideas and give workers parameters within which their ideas must fit. Once he had their ideas he could make the decision.

- ❑ Advantages:

    1) They may come up with alternatives he has not thought of.

    2) They will be committed to making their ideas work.

- ❑ Disadvantage: It takes time.

Level 4: Present the issues, give them parameters within which they must operate, and allow them to make the decision.

- ❑ Advantages:

    1) It gives them broad latitude to be creative.

    2) They may bring additional initiative, ideas, and energy to their jobs.

    3) Since it is their decision, they will be committed to making it work.

- ❑ Disadvantages:

    1) It takes time.

    2) He must live with their decisions.

After thinking about our conversation, Mike decided that he would make a radical departure from his normal way of doing things and try Level 3.

When he met with his employees, Mike explained that the team had not been meeting the objective of keeping the lines running 90% of the time. He noted that when the lines are down it costs the company money. Finally, he asked his staff to come up with ways to keep the lines running 90% of the time. The only parameter was they could not do anything that would add to the cost of running the maintenance team.

Once they got over the shock of his new approach, the technicians arranged to meet without Mike being present. A few days later they asked him to meet with them to hear what they had come up with as a way of fixing the problem.

For the first time, Mike listened to what they had to say and he learned a great deal. He learned, for example, that Fred liked working on the large machines, and that Tommy liked working on the small machines. Mike decided to appoint Fred the lead technician on the large machines and to appoint Tommy the lead technician on the small machines. In addition to volunteering to do preventive maintenance on their own time, the technicians also recommended that Mike arrange to have the company that manufactured the machines come to the plant and conduct a free seminar on the latest maintenance techniques.

Improvements were immediate. The team achieved the 90% level for the first time. But the results did not stop there. Before long, the machines were consistently running 98% of the time.

2. Routinely ask employees for their opinions.

In my first supervisory assignment, service representatives would come to me and tell me that they had a customer on the telephone whose bill was past due but that the customer wanted to wait until next Wednesday to pay the bill. I would look at the bill and ask the service representatives what they thought. Initially, they were reluctant to tell me what they thought because their previous supervisors had never asked for their opinion. Instead, they had simply told them what to tell the customer.

After some prodding, however, they would tell me (for example) that they thought we should insist on having the full payment in the public office by 5 p.m. that day or we should turn off the service. I would agree and that is what they would tell the customer.

The next step was that they would come to me and make a recommendation rather than asking me what to do. Eventually, they got to the point they would make the decision without consulting with me at all.

3. Challenge employees to come up with ways to improve the operation.

Surveys show that 85 percent of employees would be willing to give ideas about how to improve things if their supervisor asked them. One supervisor did just that and one of his employees came up with an idea that saved the company $100,000. When the supervisor asked him why he had not said something sooner he replied, "Nobody asked."

4. Conduct "Quality Circles."

Get a group of employees together once per month without your being present, give them a specific issue and have them come up with ideas for resolving it. Give them even more ownership by allowing them to pick members of the team.

5. Permit employees to participate in management meetings.

The Donnelly Corporation of Holland, Michigan has had great success worldwide for several years using this idea.

6. Conduct regular brainstorming sessions.

> "The best way to have a good idea is to have a lot of ideas."
>
> –Dr. Linus Pauling, management trainer

Since most problems are not solved by the first idea that comes to mind, it is important to consider many possible solutions. One of the best ways to do this is through brainstorming, the act of defining a problem and coming up with as many possible solutions as you can - no matter how ridiculous some of them may sound.

For best results:

a) Select a recorder.

b) Define the problem and make sure everyone agrees.

c) Establish the ground rules, i.e.

- ❑ Letting the leader have control.

- ❑ Allowing everyone to contribute.

- ❑ No insulting or demeaning of participants.

- ❑ Deferring judgment of ideas until the end.

- ❑ Encouraging "wild" ideas.

- ❑ Recording each answer.

- ❑ Building on each other's ideas.

- ❑ Staying focused on the problem.

- ❑ One conversation at a time.

- ❑ Setting a time limit.

d) Start the session at the agreed upon time.

e) Have the recorder write down all responses so everyone can see them.

f) Stop the session at the agreed upon time.

g) Evaluate the responses.

- ❑ Eliminate ideas that do not fit.

- ❑ Combine similar ideas.

- ❑ List the pros and cons of each idea.

- ❑ Select the best ideas and implement them.

7. Turn mistakes into positive learning experiences.

Employees have many ideas on how to cut costs, improve sales, and build value into your product or service. But fear of making a mistake can stifle their willingness to try something new. So if employees make a mistake, discuss what they learned and move on. As Albert Einstein said, "Anyone who has not made a mistake has never tried anything new."

8. Encourage employees to put themselves in the role of one of your customers.

They will probably identify several improvements to make the customer's experience more pleasant.

9. Give recognition for good ideas.

You may award cash or some other desirable prize.

10. Use words and phrases that indicate you want their input. Here are some examples:

a) "Before we develop the overtime policy I want to get your ideas."

b) "How do you suggest we go about setting up the work teams?"

c) "Let's formulate a strategy that meets the goal but is comfortable to both of us."

d) "How can we evaluate how we are doing throughout the year?"

e) "What is the number one hurdle you face?"

f) "Are you aware of what we are trying to achieve here?"

g) "Do you see any flaws in the process we are considering?"

h) "Would you please give this some thought and discuss it with me on Monday?"

i) "Perhaps I need to rethink my original decision."

j) "We can solve this if we work together."

k) "It is up to us to develop a workable process."

Caveats:

1. If you have already decided what you are going to do, do not ask for input. Employees will see you as insincere.

2. Seriously consider their ideas. If possible, implement them even if you have to make some modifications. For the ones you do not implement, explain why. It really turns people off to ask for their ideas and neither implement them nor explain why you did not.

3. Since some employees shy away from speaking up in group meetings, meet with them one-on-one to get their ideas.

According to people who study such things, a normal brain more than 14 billion cells and connections. This means that employees are capable of incredible creativity when it comes to making decisions and solving problems. So give them the opportunity to use their brains.

ACTION PLAN

Write any ideas you will implement within your work team.

1._____.

2._____.

3._____.

4._____.

5._____.

10

THEY ARE NOT PENALIZED FOR NOT MEETING EXPECTATIONS

Solution: Develop penalties.

How to implement the solution:

1. Provide closer supervision.

Most employees do not want to have their supervisor hovering over their shoulder. I know a supervisor who has used this to his advantage. Since he has employees spread out all over the state, he cannot possibly be with all of them at once. However, he has made it clear that if any of them fail to meet performance expectations he will devote a significant part of his day to "supervising" them. The possibility that he would actually do it is enough to deter all of them from low performance.

2. Link pay to performance.

Give pay increases and bonuses only to those employees who met performance expectations.

3. Put their Individual Development Plan (IDP) on hold.

Tell employees they forfeit the opportunity to develop and implement an IDP if their performance falls below fully satisfactory,

4. Deny employees the opportunity to attend a special class.

5. Demote them to a lower paying position.

6. Remove them from the payroll.

These are some ideas. Consider your organizational culture as well as what you know about your individual employees in determining appropriate penalties. The point is to have some penalty for performance failures.

ACTION PLAN

Write any ideas you will implement within your work team.

1._____.

2._____.

3._____.

4._____.

5._____.

Why employees fail to meet performance expectations

11

THEY ARE REWARDED FOR NOT MEETING EXPECTATIONS

Perhaps the only thing worse than not penalizing poor performance is rewarding it. Let me give you an example.

Service technicians were dispatched all over the state. The department objective was for them to finish all assigned work on the day it was assigned, without working overtime. However, if Jim's technicians had not finished their work by mid afternoon, they would call him and ask him to authorize overtime. Without doing any verification to determine the necessity, and without considering any other alternatives (assigning additional resources, negotiating a new completion date with the client, etc.), Jim always authorized the overtime. His technicians based their projected annual income on the assumption that they were going to work overtime regularly. He had fallen into the habit of not only not penalizing his employees for failing to meet performance expectations, but actually rewarding them for their failure.

Solution: Give rewards only for performance that meets or surpasses expectations.

How to implement the solution:

1. Evaluate the kinds of behavior you are rewarding.

2. Make sure there are penalties, not rewards, for behavior that does not meet expectations.

ACTION PLAN

Write any ideas you will implement within your work team.

1._____.

2._____.

3._____.

4._____.

5._____.

WHY EMPLOYEES FAIL TO MEET PERFORMANCE EXPECTATIONS

12

THEY ARE PENALIZED FOR MEETING EXPECTATIONS

Paula was an excellent teacher. She always surpassed performance expectations; her students achieved extremely high scores on standardized tests as well as on regular classroom work. As a noted disciplinarian, she did not tolerate any "foolishness" and her students respected her tremendously. She had been named outstanding teacher in her district for two consecutive years. And she was "rewarded" by being moved to the second worst performing school in the district, followed by being moved to the absolute worst school in the district the next year. Paula became a very different teacher. She did not put in the preparation time and generally took the attitude, "I am just here for the paycheck." Paula had slid into the abyss known as mediocrity.

Let us look at another example. Sally and Jim were claims adjusters for an insurance company. Sally was an eager beaver, worked diligently to finish all of her claims on time and always had all of the necessary documentation in order. On the other hand, Jim slacked off, did not finish his claims on time and often had to redo his documentation because of multiple errors and or omissions.

In order to meet deadlines, Tom, Jim and Sally's supervisor, often assigned some of Jim's cases to Sally for her to complete. Yet, year after year, the two of them earned the same salary and received the same bonuses.

As management consultant Bob Talbert said, "Busy workers are happy workers – until they find out that the lazy workers are paid the same or more."

It was not long before Sally realized that there was no real advantage to putting in so much extra effort. She began to think, "Why should I work hard and even take on some of Jim's work if he does much less and not only gets away with it but gets paid the same thing I do?" Pretty soon, both the quality and the quantity of her work began to suffer.

Both Paula and Sally were, in effect, penalized for being outstanding performers. As a result, both began performing at a much lower level.

Solution: Never penalize employees who meet or exceed performance expectations.

How to implement the solution:

1. Evaluate the kinds of behavior you are penalizing.

2. Make sure there are rewards, not penalties, for behavior that meets the expectations.

ACTION PLAN

Write any ideas you will implement within your work team.

1._____.

2._____.

3._____.

4._____.

5._____.

13

THEY DON'T BELIEVE THEY CAN MEET EXPECTATIONS

It is not unusual for employees to doubt their ability to perform their duties well enough to meet performance expectations. This is most likely to happen if they are new to the work team or have been assigned new responsibilities.

Solution: Boost their self-esteem.

"Outstanding leaders go out of their way to boost the self-esteem of their employees. If people believe in themselves it's amazing what they can do."

–Sam Walton, founder of Wal-Mart

How to implement the solution:

1. Assure your workers that you have confidence in them.

2. Focus on successes they have had.

Encourage them to think about success they have had in school, previous work assignments, athletics, service to others, etc. Point out the skills they used in achieving that success and how they can use those same skills to achieve success in the current environment.

3. Assign a mentor.

A mentor can show new employees the ropes and help them make the transition to the group a seamless one.

4. Limit the number of duties you initially assign.

Let us take the example of an Office Services Assistant. The total duties might be:

- ❏ Prepare travel reports.

- ❏ Answer the telephone.

- ❏ Direct walk-in applicants.

You could have the employee begin by preparing travel reports. Once he or she becomes proficient at that, you can add the other two duties.

5. Be available for coaching.

Initiate regular meetings to give feedback, offer encouragement, and to identify and remove any obstacles.

6. Have employees "progress" toward the ultimate goal.

Company president Alfred J. Marrow was interested in having his newly hired factory employees become fully productive as soon as possible. So he decided to conduct an experiment. He broke the new hires into two groups.

With group one, he immediately set the objective at the level of an experienced factory worker. He then told the workers that he expected them to reach it within 12 weeks after they were hired.

After 14 weeks, this group had only achieved 66 percent of the objective of an experienced factory worker.

With the second group of new hires, Mr. Marrow set objectives for them to achieve each week. The first week the objectives were very low. Each week, as the employees became more competent and confident, Mr. Marrow raised the objective slightly over what it had been the previous week. The results were startling. After 14 weeks the average member of the group had reached 100 percent of the objectives of an experienced factory worker.

In your case, let's say the ultimate goal is to get to 98% accuracy. You could begin the year at, say, 95% and increase it until by the 4th quarter of the year the goal is 98%. As with Mr. Marrow's employees, your staff will experience some success and they will gain confidence as they go. The end result will be a higher level of performance.

ACTION PLAN

Write any ideas you will implement within your work team.

1._____.

2._____.

3._____.

4._____.

5._____.

14

THEY DON'T HAVE THE PROPER TOOLS, EQUIPMENT OR SUPPLIES

Surveys show that the lack of proper tools, equipment and supplies can reduce employee productivity by as much as 30 percent. Let me give you an example of how this can happen:

Janet had been the front office assistant for two years. Her duties consisted of answering the telephone, greeting visitors, directing them to the appropriate staff person and making copies for the staff. Recently, since she had been away from her desk an awful lot, she had not available to greet and direct visitors.

After observing this for a while Marvin, Janet's supervisor, met with her to find out why she was away from her desk so much. Janet explained that for quite some time she had been going to the third floor to make copies. That arrangement had been working fine since she had been able to go up, make the copies and quickly return to her desk. However, the third floor supervisor had recently installed a new copier that was much faster than the old one. Since others had found out about the new high-speed copier they, too, were going to the third floor to make their copies.

As a result, instead of just running up, quickly making her copies, and returning to her desk, Janet found herself having to wait in line.

Solution: Provide the proper tools, equipment and supplies.

How to implement the solution:

1. Observe your employees in action to see if they have what they need to perform their duties effectively and efficiently.

It may be helpful to examine Figure 14.1 - Sample Checklist to get some ideas on the kinds of things that may need.

2. Bridge the gap between what they have and what they need.

Marvin's solution was to install a small copier right across from Janet's desk. Since she can now make copies without leaving the floor, Janet is available to greet all visitors.

Figure 14.1

SAMPLE CHECKLIST

Tools

- ❑ Hammer
- ❑ Wrenches
- ❑ Pliers
- ❑ Other

Equipment

- ❑ Computer
- ❑ Telephone
- ❑ Fax machine
- ❑ Copier
- ❑ Scales
- ❑ Postage meter
- ❑ Other

Supplies

- ❑ Pencils/pens
- ❑ Stapler
- ❑ Ruler
- ❑ Letter opener
- ❑ Reference material
- ❑ Other

Furniture

- ❑ Comfortable chair
- ❑ Desk
- ❑ Other

ACTION PLAN

Write any ideas you will implement within your work team.

1._____.

2._____.

3._____.

4._____.

5._____.

15

THEY ARE BORED

"A number of problems in business and industry are the result of boredom."

–Dr. Pat McCarthy, Industrial Psychologist

Employees consistently say they want interesting work to do. However, in many cases they say they are bored. This could be because their work never challenged them or perhaps they have performed the same tasks for a long time.

Solution: Find ways to eliminate boredom.

How to implement the solution:

1. Assign them to a different existing position.

This gives them opportunities to learn new skills and face some new challenges.

2. Create a new position.

Carl had been a mailroom clerk for three years. Eileen, Carl's supervisor, had seen his productivity drop dramatically over the previous six months.

During her mid-year performance review with Carl, she pointed out that drop-off and asked him for an explanation.

When Carl indicated that after three years of performing the same tasks he had become frustrated and bored, and said he was even thinking about looking for another job, Eileen knew she needed to do something. She asked him about his interests. When Carl said he liked working with numbers Eileen began thinking about the mountain of paperwork in her office that was related to vendor invoices. She decided to make Carl the billing specialist for the department. In his new position, he was responsible for analyzing all vendor bills and either certifying their accuracy or investigating discrepancies. Carl loved this new assignment and he was very effective. During the next six months, he saved the company more than $100,000 by identifying duplicate charges.

3. Enlarge their existing position.

Since surveys show that 85 percent of employees think their boss underutilizes them, you could expand a worker's tasks without increasing his or her level of authority. This is called horizontal job enrichment.

Mike Ditka, the former coach of the Chicago Bears, understands this concept. During the 1980s, Coach Ditka had a defensive tackle named William "The Refrigerator" Perry. While Perry was effective, he sometimes became bored with the rather mundane existence of a defensive tackle. When he got bored, he overate, gained excess weight and lost some of his effectiveness.

As an incentive for keeping his weight under control, Coach Ditka decided to allow The "Refrigerator" to play on the offensive side of the ball in certain situations.

He got to carry the ball and he even scored a few touchdowns. The Bears went on to win the 1985 Super Bowl.

4. Give employees more authority.

With this arrangement you may or may not increase the number of tasks. However, you give workers more decision-making authority. This is called vertical job enrichment.

Let me give you an example. Geraldine worked as a claims representative. David, the team leader, reviewed each claim that she and the other representatives prepared. He highlighted errors and returned the claim to the originator for correction. Since Geraldine had not had an error in six months, David gave her the authority to evaluate all of the claims from the work team and decide if they should be returned for correction or should be sent directly to the accounting department.

Whether you are considering enlarging or enriching employees' jobs it is a good idea to get their input by:

a) Having them complete Figure 15.1 - Employee Interest Questionnaire.

b) Meeting with them to discuss their answers to the questions.

Note: You may want to eliminate or reassign some of their existing duties in order to free up time to allow them to perform the enlarged or enriched duties.

As motivational theorist Frederick Herzberg said, "If you want people to be motivated to do a good job, give them a good job to do."

5. Act as a career counselor.

At least once per year I would ask my employees where they wanted to be in three years. The first time I did it, they were shocked because no one had asked them about their aspirations before. Once they got over the shock, they began establishing career goals.

6. Encourage employees to prepare an Individual Development Plan (IDP). (See Figure 15.2).

By helping employees improve weaknesses, build on strengths and improve job performance, an IDP can help them reach their career goals within the context of organizational objectives. Steps of the IDP process:

Step 1 – Self-Assessment and initial draft of goals

a) Employees should review their prior job experience, training/education, and developmental activities. This provides concrete information regarding current strengths and skills.

b) They should evaluate their current job performance. This involves a review of performance with an honest assessment of weaknesses that you and prior supervisors have pointed out.

c) They should draft initial career goals and research the developmental opportunities required to reach these goals. These may include special assignments, self-study courses, and formal training.

Step 2 – Employee/Supervisor Meeting

Objective: To obtain a mutual commitment between you and the employees regarding the IDP plan.

a) They are responsible for arranging a meeting with you to discuss their needs in the context of the job requirements. Topics for discussion include their strengths and weaknesses, current job duties and responsibilities, organizational needs, time and financial resources, and learning opportunities that you will actively support.

b) You can coach them by providing information about the organization's mission, career paths, and a reasonable time frame in which to accomplish their goals.

Step 3 – Finalization and Implementation

Objective: To actively follow through on the IDP commitment.

a) The employees make changes and prepare the final IDP. You and the employees sign the IDP form indicating support of the plan. The employees keep the original IDP and give you a copy.

b) The employees implement the development plan by submitting training requests, participating in activities, and giving you updates on any changes.

Step 4 – Follow-up and Review

Objective: To make the IDP a systematic, ongoing process, which supports the employees' career development needs.

The employees should routinely update and review the plan and meet with you every six months to determine progress and to make any required changes.

Caveat: You should point out to the employees that, while the IDP can help prepare them to become qualified for a higher graded position, it does not imply a guarantee of advancement.

7. Establish a job rotation system.

Allow employees to rotate to other jobs inside and outside of your department to learn new skills.

8. Create a shadowing program.

Allow them to observe other employees to learn new skills.

9. Establish personal development accounts.

Set aside a specific amount of money for employees to use as they see fit on any other work-related activity, i.e. attending training, ordering books or tapes, going to a conference, etc.

10. Provide cross training.

Provide training on other functions within the department.

11. Implement a mentoring program.

Allow experienced employees to train (mentor) newer employees. Provide special training for the mentors to prepare them for the role.

12. Provide opportunities for formal education.

Encourage employees to use the tuition reimbursement program to attend college. Allow them to work a flexible schedule to meet class/homework commitments.

13. Allow employees to make presentations to the team.

This provides a chance for improving presentation skills.

For example, after someone has attended an outside seminar or workshop you could have them brief the other employees regarding seminar content and highlights.

14. Have employees lead a project team.

15. Give them a copy of my book, *Paddle Your Own Boat: 10 Rules that Guarantee Career Success.*

Order the book at www.vernonwilliams.net.

16. Institute skill-based pay.

Increase the pay for employees with a higher degree of job-related skills and certifications.

17. Allow employees to fill in for you.

Have employees attend some meetings that you would normally attend. Have them run the group during your absence.

18. Encourage employees to become active in your industry's trade association.

19. Delegate special assignments.

Before delegating you should determine:

a) The name of the task.

b) Why it is important.

c) The outcome you expect. It should be:

- ❑ Specific: What do you want?

- ❑ Measurable: How will you know if you received what you wanted?

- ❑ Accountable: The delegate must accept accountability for delivering what you want.

- ❑ Realistic: It has to be possible for the delegate to achieve what you want. _

- ❑ Time Definite: Establish a firm date of when you want the outcome.

d) Why you chose him/her. (Match skills to the task's requirements.)

e) The start and completion dates.

f) The decision-making authority.

How much latitude do delegatees have to make decisions? What should they do if they need a decision made that exceeds their authority?

g) The available resources.

What equipment, supplies, space, reference material, people and money are available to the delegatees?

h) The follow-up dates.

These are the dates you will meet with the delegatees to measure progress, identify roadblocks, and determine if additional resources are needed, etc.

You can use Figure 15.3 - Delegation Worksheet at the end of this chapter to delegate assignments.

Note: It may also be necessary to eliminate/assign to another employee (at least temporarily) some of the delegatee's current duties.

20. Inject a heavy dose of fun.

"A happy employee is a more productive employee, so I want my employees to be happy."

–Zane Tankel, president, Collier Graphics

If you have ever seen Sammy Sosa hit a home run you have seen someone who truly enjoys his job. Sosa hops high into the air and instantly goes into an airplane mode, running to first with his arms extended outward like a little kid in his back yard. Perhaps the fact that Sosa has so much fun has helped him move up to number 8 on the all-time list of home run hitters.

Some ways to have fun:

a) Sponsor an office softball team.

You could play against other companies or agencies.

b) Have a weird hat day.

Award a prize to the person who shows up wearing the weirdest hat.

c) Have meetings in unusual places.

Have meetings off-site. I used to have staff meetings at a park during the spring and summer. We wore shorts and T-shirts and we played volleyball during our lunch break.

d) Have theme parties.

Memorial Day, the 4th of July, Labor Day, Halloween, are just some of the holidays around which you can build a theme.

e) Put up seasonal decorations.

f) Have bagels one morning per week.

g) Have Friday afternoon sundaes.

h) Have an office cookout.

i) Set up a "Fun Committee."

This creates ownership among the employees and insures that the activities are appropriate for your organization.

j) Give an award that requires you to dress up in a funny costume.

k) Encourage employees to develop a skit to reenact something funny that has happened at work.

l) Decorate the walls with funny posters.

m) Put up photos of employees when they were high school seniors.

n) Celebrate employees' birthdays.

In one of my offices the person who had the previous birthday was responsible for bringing in a cake for the person who had the next birthday. This worked well because it got everyone involved. On the day of the birthday all of us gathered around and sang (not very well) "Happy Birthday."

o) Sponsor a golf tournament on company time.

p) Organize an employee talent show.

q) Sponsor a chili-cooking contest.

r) Organize a potluck lunch.

These are obviously just a few ideas. Feel free to create your own. The goal is to have fun. It will have a huge impact on your employees and, in turn, your customers. Let me give you an example of how a happy employee can impact customers.

Reggie Wilson drives a bus in Seattle. It's a thankless job filled with stress, time pressures and difficult customers. Yet Reggie is a happy employee who not only delivers the best possible service but, by singing and smiling, he makes his customers smile, too.

One woman told a very personal story about the time she was on her way home from the hospital after a chemotherapy appointment. She was weak but she braved the rain and waited an extra 20 minutes for Reggie's bus. She said that the energy he gave her and the happiness she felt that day made a big difference in her recovery.

Figure 15.1

EMPLOYEE INTEREST QUESTIONNAIRE

1. What skills do you have that you don't use?

2. What skills do you like to use most?

3. In what area(s) would you like increased responsibility?

4. If you could, in what ways would you change your job?

Figure 15.2

INDIVIDUAL DEVELOPMENT PLAN (IDP)

Employee Name:_____

Department:_____

Position Title:_____

Employment Date:_____

Section One - Training and Self-development History

Education Level (Circle highest level completed):

9 10 11 12 13 14 15 16

Major field of study_____

College courses completed (If no degree):

Training courses completed:

Other training (trade, vocational, business):

Figure 15.2 - Page 2

INDIVIDUAL DEVELOPMENT PLAN (IDP)

Section Two – Employment History

(List positions in reverse chronological order)

Dates	Position Title	Employer

Section Three – Community Activities

(Briefly describe any activities that you consider pertinent
to your career development, e.g. PTA, served on the
community association board, etc.)

_____

_____

_____

Section Four – Licenses and Certifications

_____

_____

_____

Figure 15.2 - Page 3

INDIVIDUAL DEVELOPMENT PLAN (IDP)

Section Five – Career Objectives

A. Short range (within two years) objectives:

_____

_____

_____

Skills needed in order to accomplish those objectives:

_____

_____

_____

B. Long-range (three years and beyond) objectives:

_____

_____

_____

Skills needed in order to accomplish those objectives:

_____

_____

_____

They are bored

127

Figure 15.2 - Page 4

INDIVIDUAL DEVELOPMENT PLAN (IDP)

Section Six – Training to be completed to develop needed skills

Course   Dates

_____

_____

_____

Section Seven – Education to be completed to develop needed skills

College/University   Course   Dates

_____

_____

_____

Section Eight – Work activities to develop needed skills

Work activity   Dates

_____

_____

_____

Figure 15.2 - Page 5

INDIVIDUAL DEVELOPMENT PLAN (IDP)

Employee's Signature _____

Date_____

Supervisor's Signature _____

Date_____

Figure 15.3

DELEGATION WORKSHEET

1. Name of the task: _____

2. Why the task is important: _____

3. Outcome you expect: _____

4. Why you chose him/her: _____

5. Start and completion dates: _____

6. Decision-making authority: _____

7. Available resources: _____

8. Follow-up dates: _____

ACTION PLAN

Write any ideas you will implement within your work team.

1._____.

2._____.

3._____.

4._____.

5._____.

16

THEY THINK WHAT THEY DO IS NOT IMPORTANT

As a library assistant, Jane was responsible for placing new books on the shelves within two days of their arrival. Gladys, Jane's supervisor, noticed that recently Jane had not only been falling short of that objective, but she was also placing some books in the wrong sections. When Gladys spoke to her about these deficiencies, Jane said she did not think that what she did was all that important. She is not alone. Surveys show that 61 percent of employees feel exactly the same way.

Solution: Point out the importance of what they do.

"People must believe that a task is inherently worthwhile if they are to be committed to it."

–Edward Deci, author and management consultant

How to implement the solution:

1. Review your organization's mission statement and goals with the employees.

2. Relate their job function to your organization's mission statement and goals.

Gladys reviewed the library's mission statement with Jane:

> "Our mission is to inform, enrich and empower every person in our community by creating and promoting easy access to a vast array of information. We will acquire, organize and provide books and other relevant materials; serve our public with expert and caring assistance; and reach out to all members of our community."

Gladys pointed out that Jane's job was critically important in providing "Easy access to a wide array of information." Once Jane fully understood the importance of her role, Gladys noticed a big improvement in both the quality and quantity of Jane's work.

3. Tell employees success stories about people who benefit from your work group's product or service.

4. Post "thank You" letters from customers on the bulletin board, web site, in the employee lounge and/or other conspicuous locations.

5. Show them how meeting performance objectives will help them achieve their personal/professional goals.

6. Include them in designing the work process, making decisions and solving problems.

ACTION PLAN

Write any ideas you will implement within your work team.

1. _____.

2. _____.

3. _____.

4. _____.

5. _____.

WHY EMPLOYEES FAIL TO MEET PERFORMANCE EXPECTATIONS

17

THE SUPERVISOR HAS LOW EXPECTATIONS

The Baltimore Ravens used their first draft choice in 2002 to select Kyle Boller, a strong-armed quarterback from the University of California. Kyle began the 2003 season as the starting quarterback. However, the coaches told him they had a great defense and a strong running game so all he had to do was not make mistakes that would cause them to lose. To further minimize the chances that he would make errors the coaches reduced the playbook to a few simple plays.

When the season got underway, Kyle had little confidence, made several mistakes, and in general did not perform well. The team stumbled under his leadership but had a successful season because, after Boller was injured, the backup quarterback, Anthony Wright, took over and led them to the playoffs.

In 2003, The Pittsburgh Steelers drafted Ben Rothlisberger, a quarterback from the University of Miami of Ohio. The team's plan was to use him as the backup his first year. But when starting quarterback Tommy Maddox was injured, Ben stepped into the starting lineup.

Instead of telling Ben not to lose, the coaches told him they had complete confidence in him and that they expected him to lead the team as well as the more experienced Tommy Maddox had done prior to his injury.

They also allowed Ben to run all the same plays that Tommy Maddox had run. As a result, the Steelers won 13 games in a row, Ben threw 17 touchdown passes and had a quarterback rating of 98.1 percent, and the Steelers made the playoffs.

These stories illustrate what is known as the Pygmalion effect, which has the following key principles:

1) Leaders form certain expectations of employees.

It was clear that the Baltimore coaches had low expectations for Kyle Boller, while the Pittsburgh coaches had high expectations for Ben Rothlisberger.

2) Leaders communicate those expectations to employees.

The coaches communicated those expectations. In Boller's case, they told him to run simple plays and not make mistakes. In Rothlisberger's case, they expressed complete confidence in him and expected him to perform as proficiently as the more experienced quarterback.

3) Employees pick up on the leader's expectations.

Both Boller and Rothlisberger recognized their coaches' expectations.

4) Employees adjust their behavior to match their leader's expectations.

While Boller floundered, Rothlisberger flourished.

Solution: Set high expectations.

How to implement the solution:

1. Set demanding objectives that cause the employees to stretch. (See Cause #3 – Set Performance Goals).

In doing so, you are saying to your employees that you believe they can make a positive contribution to the team. This helps them improve their self-concept and thus their self-esteem. They will believe they can succeed, will have higher expectations for themselves and will perform at a higher level.

2. If they make a mistake, offer corrective feedback instead of criticism.

3. Provide support and encouragement as needed.

4. Avoid giving praise for performance that fails to meet expectations.

This reinforces unwanted behavior and increases the likelihood that they will repeat it.

ACTION PLAN

Write any ideas you will implement within your work team.

1. _____ .

2. _____ .

3. _____ .

4. _____ .

5. _____ .

18

THE SUPERVISOR IS MEASURING PRODUCTIVITY IMPROPERLY

When I was appointed assistant sales manager, I wanted to "hit the ground running." I decided to measure productivity based on the number of appointments that my sales representatives completed. My thinking was the more appointments they went out on, the more sales they would make. That makes sense, right?

Wrong.

I quickly found out that, even though the sales representatives were exceeding the objective for the number of appointments, they were making very few sales.

That reminded me of a story that I had heard, The Beekeepers and their Bees.

Once upon a time, there were two beekeepers who managed beehives for a company called Bees, Inc. The company's customers loved their honey so much they wanted them to produce more than they had the previous year. So upper management told the beekeepers to increase their production by 25% over the previous year, but to maintain the same quality.

The first beekeeper never told the bees that the objective was to produce more honey so that Bees, Inc., could increase honey sales. Instead he told them he was going to measure the number of flowers each bee visited. At midseason, he provided feedback to the bees on their individual performance, and he gave out special awards for the bees that visited the most flowers.

The second beekeeper took a different approach. He immediately told each bee that the goal was to produce 25% more honey than they had the previous year, but to maintain the same quality. He also told them he would measure the amount of nectar that each of them delivered and the amount of honey the hive produced. He charted each bee's performance and the hive's overall performance and posted the results on the bulletin board. He also created awards. But unlike the first beekeeper, he based the awards on the amount of nectar they gathered and on the hive's production of honey--the more honey produced the more recognition each bee received.

At the end of the season, the beekeepers evaluated their results. The first beekeeper found that his hive had indeed increased the number of flowers visited, but the amount of honey the hive produced was actually less than it had been the previous year. The Queen Bee reported that because the bees had been so busy trying to visit as many flowers as possible, they had limited the amount of nectar they would carry so they could fly faster.

One bee told the beekeeper that if he had told them that the real objective was to make more honey rather than to visit more flowers, he would have done his work completely differently.

The second beekeeper had very different results. Because each bee in his hive was focused on the hive's objective of producing 25% more honey, the bees had concentrated their efforts on gathering more nectar to produce more honey than ever before. They had identified the highest nectar-yielding flowers and had created quicker processes for depositing the nectar they'd gathered. Not surprisingly, the hive reached its objective of producing 25% more honey than it had the previous year, while maintaining the same quality. The beekeeper awarded each bee the recognition he had promised.

Although it somewhat oversimplifies performance management, the story illustrates an important point. The first beekeeper had measured activities - visiting flowers, while the second beekeeper had measured accomplishments - the amount of nectar delivered and the amount honey the hive produced.

Solution: Measure accomplishments, not activities.

How to implement the solution:

1. Define "activities" as they relate to your work team.

"Activities" are the actions your employees take to produce results and are generally described using verbs. In the beekeeper story, the activity was visiting flowers.

Examples of activities in your case may include:

❑ Filing documents.

❑ Developing software programs.

- ❏ Answering customer questions.

- ❏ Writing reports.

2. Define "accomplishments" as they relate to your work team.

"Accomplishments" are the products or services produced and are generally described using nouns. The amount of nectar each bee collected and the honey production are examples of accomplishments in the beehive story. Examples in your case may include:

- ❏ Files that are orderly and complete.

- ❏ A software program that works.

- ❏ Accurate guidance to customers.

- ❏ A report that is complete and accurate.

3. Measure the items you listed in Item 2.

I realized that since I wanted to support the organizational goals, I needed to use the second beekeeper's approach of measuring and rewarding accomplishments rather than activities. The accomplishment I was looking for was increased sales revenue. I really did not care if the sales representatives made one appointment or twenty appointments.

After getting some input from the sales representatives, we changed the measurement from the number of appointments to a specific amount of revenue I expected them to generate for the company.

Guess what? Once we had the correct measurement in place, the sales representatives met their revenue objective, which was the whole point in the first place.

ACTION PLAN

Write any ideas you will implement within your work team.

1. _____ .

2. _____ .

3. _____ .

4. _____ .

5. _____ .

19

THEY HAVE "ISSUES" WITH THE SUPERVISOR

"Good hours, excellent pay, fun place to work, paid training, mean boss. Oh well, four out of five isn't bad."

–Help wanted ad

Employees often point to their relationship with their supervisor as a prime reason they are not performing up to expectations and, indeed, in their decision to stay with or to leave an organization.

Solution: Take steps to prevent "issues".

How to implement the solution:

1. Earn employees' trust.

Trust is the most important element in building a positive work environment. In fact, 54% of employees surveyed said they were willing to work for slightly less money if high trust factors were present in the workplace.

How to earn employees' trust:

a) Make sure you have basic supervisory skills.

Employees will never trust you if they perceive you are inept at the fundamentals of managing. These fundamentals include:

- ❑ Establishing objectives.

- ❑ Assigning work.

- ❑ Monitoring performance.

- ❑ Working effectively with subordinates from a variety of backgrounds.

- ❑ Planning your personal work and carrying out assignments effectively.

- ❑ Communicating effectively both orally and in writing.

- ❑ Analyzing and solving problems.

b) Make sure you are knowledgeable about all aspects of their work.

It is difficult for employees to trust you if they do not believe you understand what they do.

c) Give them some decision-making power.

Since adults need to feel some degree of control over their environment, let them participate in decisions that impact them.

d) Do not allow employee "A" to come to you and complain about employee "B."

Encourage them to work it out. However, if the issue affects productivity, you may want to call them together and try to mediate a resolution.

e) Protect employees' interests.

Keep private conversations private. Do not talk to employee "A" about employee "B." Do not place blame or publicly point fingers when there are performance failures.

f) Treat all employees fairly.

It is extremely difficult to build trust if employees believe that you are showing favoritism. Let's say two employees (Sally and George) come to work late. You verbally reprimand George but say nothing to Sally. Is that fair? What message does that send? Make sure you dole out assistance, coaching, rewards and punishment equitably. I should point out that treating employees fairly does not necessarily mean treating them all the same. I remember a reporter asking Rev. Jesse Jackson if he treated all of his children the same. He said he did not treat them all the same, but he treated them all fairly. I agree with that answer.

Let me give you an example of how I did not treat all of my employees the same, but I treated them fairly.

I worked for a company in which there was a policy that prohibited employees from making or receiving personal telephone calls while at their desk. There was a lounge with several telephones for them to make or receive calls before work, during the morning break, at lunchtime, during the afternoon break or after work.

However, one of my employees was a single mom with a middle school daughter. I allowed her to receive a call from her daughter each day after school to let her know she was home safely.

The other employees did not object because I had made exceptions to accommodate others with special needs.

Another way to avoid the perception of favoritism is, instead of turning to the same person for help all the time, spread the opportunities around.

g) Stand up for employees.

Be an advocate for your employees. Showing public support lets them know you "have their back," and in turn they will believe in you and trust you.

h) Be available.

Make yourself available to help with any work or personal issues they encounter.

i) Be consistent.

Employees should be able to predict how you are going to react in every situation. This gives them a feeling of confidence. If circumstances change, as they might, explain why you are reacting differently.

j) Keep your word.

If you tell them you are going to do something, follow through on the promise. This applies to things like keeping appointments, providing training, making changes in work assignments, providing assistance, getting an answer to a question from Human Resources, etc. Failure to do so sends a message that you are all talk and no action. Never make promises you can't keep.

k) Admit your mistakes.

The six most important words in the English language are, "I admit I made a mistake." If you make a mistake, rather than trying to explain it away, admit it. That shows a human quality to which employees can relate.

l) Admit if you don't know something.

If employees ask you a question and you don't know the answer say, "I do not know the answer. However, I will have an answer for you tomorrow." Then, of course, you need to keep your promise by giving them the answer. If you need more time to do research, let them know and schedule a new commitment date.

m) Tell the truth, the whole truth and nothing but the truth.

Always tell your employees the truth, even if it is not what they want to hear. If you try to hide information it will always catch up with you.

n) Ask employees for their opinion.

The four most important words in the English language are, "What is your opinion?"

o) Give trust to get trust.

Removing unnecessary audits of their work tells them that you trust them and, in turn, they are more likely to trust you.

Let me give you an example of a leader giving trust. National Football League (NFL) coaches typically force all of the players to stay in dormitories during training camp. They also impose a curfew. However, Brian Billick, the coach of the Baltimore Ravens, operates differently. He allows his veteran players to go home at night. It says to them, "I trust you to be responsible. I believe you will get your proper rest, take care of yourself and be ready to go tomorrow."

As a result players play hard for him. By the way, the Ravens won the Super Bowl in 2000.

As Rob LeBow said, "When people feel trusted they will do almost anything under the sun not to disappoint the person who has given them the gift of trust."

p) Discipline individuals, not the entire team.

If one employee is violating the organization dress code, misusing company property, etc. deal with that person individually rather than sending a threatening email or imposing a rule for the entire group.

q) Find out what employees expect from you.

Expectations go both ways. Just as your employees need to know what you expect from them, ask them what they expect from you.

r) Show appreciation.

Look for opportunities to show appreciation. When you see your employees doing something positive give them a verbal "high five" right on the spot. They will appreciate that and will trust you more.

s) Treat them with respect.

"At Marriott we know that if we treat our employees correctly, they'll treat the customers right. And if they treat the customers right, they'll keep coming back."

–Bill Marriott, chairman of the Marriott Corporation

Statistics prove that employees treat their customers the way their employer treats them.

I know of a middle school principal who requires all teachers to report to the office and sign in before they go to their classroom. Since they are professionals they feel like the principal is not treating them with respect. Yet he expects them to respect him. Employees cannot give something they don't get any more than they can come back from where they have not been. So if you want your employees to respect (and trust) you, you must respect them.

Some simple ways to showing respect are allowing them some freedoms, making requests rather than giving orders, saying "please" and "thank you".

t) Avoid unnecessary rules.

As John Madden, the former Oakland Raiders coach said, "The more rules you have, the more opportunities there are for someone to break one." His only rules were be on time and pay attention. Incidentally, Coach Madden won seven division titles, a Super Bowl and finished his career with the highest winning percentage (.750) of any coach with 100 games or more.

u) Eliminate multiple inspections and audits.

You have to do some inspections to insure quality, provide feedback and give recognition. At the same time, you do not want to get into "overkill" and to send the message that you do not trust your workers.

v) Share the spotlight.

If you take all the credit for your team's accomplishments you will surely turn off your staffers. Instead, reflect all credit to the team. Former Alabama coach Paul "Bear" Bryant, one of the most successful coaches in college football history, used to have a simple formula for getting his players to win games for him. He said:

❑   If anything goes bad, I did it.

❑   If anything goes semi-good, then we did it.

❑   If anything goes real good, then they did it.

w) Share information.

Despite all of the ways to disseminate information - cell phones, Internet, Intranet, e-mail, personal digital assistants, pagers, etc. - employees still complain about a lack of information. In fact, in a recent survey 84 percent of them said they thought they could improve their performance if management gave them more information.

Share things with them like:

1) What's going on in the organization. (Sales, opening new stores, how pending legislation or presidential initiatives might impact the agency in general and them in particular.)

2) How their job fits into the organization's mission.

3) How the organization's success will help them achieve their personal/professional goals.

4) How management arrived at a decision.

5) Progress on major organizational initiatives.

6) Results of customer satisfaction surveys.

I used to hold a monthly meeting with the entire office to go over customer satisfaction results from the previous month. It was a great opportunity to share information, offer praise and to ask for ideas on how we might improve the quality of our service.

2. Listen to employees.

According to surveys, 4 out of 10 employees say their supervisor does not listen to them.

Listening has been defined as the thoughtful, focused and active process of receiving verbal and nonverbal symbols and assigning meaning to them. Benefits of listening:

- ❑ You will have a firm grasp on how everybody feels.

- ❑ You can deal with concerns before they become major problems.

- ❑ Employees feel valued, which improves their productivity and reduces turnover.

❑ Employees become more attentive and responsive to your concerns.

a) Turn to the next page and do a quick listening self-assessment. On a scale from 1 to 3, give yourself a score as follows: 1 = never, 2 = sometimes, 3 = very often.

The higher your score the more effective you are as a listener.

Behavior	Score
I stop talking when someone is speaking to me.	
I look the person in the eye.	
I listen to the complete message without interrupting.	
I resist the temptation to finish the other person's sentences.	
I observe nonverbal clues.	
I ask open-ended questions to clarify my understanding of the message.	
Before stating my position I make sure I understand the other person's point of view.	
I listen to others' point of view even if I think they are morons.	
I maintain an open mind.	
I do not allow potential distractions to divert my attention.	
Total (Add up your scores)	

If your score is:	You are:
10 – 15	A non-listener.
16 – 23	A passive listener.
24 – 30	An empathetic listener.

b) Reasons for not listening effectively.

1) You are not interested.

2) You are busy thinking of your response.

Studies show that the average person spends approximately 65 percent of the "listening" time thinking of what he or she is going to say. So we pretend to listen and assume that we understand.

3) Listening is hard work.

Since listening involves concentration, after we listen we should feel tired. In fact, studies show that effective listening increases both the pulse rate and blood pressure.

4) You can listen faster than people can talk.

The average person can listen at a rate of 400 to 600 words per minute; most people speak at a rate of 200 to 300 words per minute. As a result, we sometimes take mental trips (daydream) and come in for the occasional landing. While we are away we could miss a key piece of information.

5) Information overload.

Several things compete for our attention. Therefore, we sometimes put up a filter to block out things we don't need. In the course of doing that, we may block out things we do need.

6) Bias.

The person may have a reputation for whining, for example.

7) You are busy.

You may be preoccupied with an upcoming meeting, getting to your in-basket, finishing a report that is due, or any one of a number of other issues.

c) How to listen effectively:

1. Take appropriate nonverbal steps such as:

❑ Turning down the music.

❑ Putting your telephone on mute.

❑ Facing the employee.

❑ Establishing eye contact.

❑ Relaxing your posture.

❑ Nodding.

2. Notice the words.

❑ Words make up 7% of the message we receive.

3. Observe the body language.

❑ Body language makes up the largest part (55%) of the message. (See Figure 19.1 for some generally accepted meanings of various body movements in the American culture.)

4. Pay attention to the vocal tone.

❑ This makes up 38% of the message.

You have probably heard people say, "It's not what you said, it's how you said it." I can remember my mother saying to me "Young man, don't you use that tone of voice with me."

5. Ask open-ended questions.

This allows you to probe for information, ideas and feelings. An example is: "Could you tell me more about why you believe that your way would work better?"

6. Offer encouraging statements.

Examples are "Uh-huh," "I see," "That's interesting," "Tell me more," and "It sounds like you have some definite ideas on the subject."

7. Let the employee know you understand the facts.

Say things like "In other words, what you have decided is ...," or "If I understand you correctly you believe that..."

8. Let the employee know you understand his/her feelings.

Examples are, "You felt left out of the loop," or "You feel that you had a better idea."

9. Summarize the key points.

Ways to do that: "These appear to be your key concerns," or "You would like to see the following changes take place."

10. Avoid:

   a) Interrupting.

   b) Forming your response while they are talking.

   c) Anticipating what they are going to say.

   d) Arguing.

   e) Judging.

   Examples of judging are, "You shouldn't feel that way," "You are making a big thing out of nothing," or "That is a dumb idea."

Let me give you an example of the impact of listening.

Recently, I was talking with Donald, a federal government supervisor who had attended one of my seminars last year. While at the seminar Donald had told me that one of his employees (Marge) had really been performing poorly. Donald's solution had been to ignore Marge. I had suggested that he engage her and find out what was at the root of her performance failure. Donald took my advice.

He arranged a meeting with Marge and for the first time he actually listened to what she had to say. It turned out that she had some solid ideas on how to make herself and the work group more effective.

Donald implemented a couple of Marge's suggestions, but more importantly, for the first time she felt like someone cared enough to listen. Donald went on to tell me that the group's performance in general, and Marge's performance in particular, had improved to the point that he had been promoted to a GS-12 position.

3. Confront poor performance head-on.

Almost every work team has some employees who fall short of performance expectations. If you continually accept that poor performance you risk alienating good performers.

They may not believe that you know who is performing well and who is performing poorly, or they may believe that you are playing favorites. In either case, they will lose trust in you as a supervisor and say, "If Joe gets away with performing poorly, why should I work hard at performing well?"

Studies show that two out of three employees believe their supervisor tolerates poor performance from some employees.

How to confront poor performance:

a) Do not assume that you are powerless.

Sometimes government supervisors tell me that, since it is extremely difficult to fire employees, if someone decides to be ROAD kill (government term for someone who is "Retired On Active Duty") they are powerless to do anything about it.

I tell them I have lots of examples in which other supervisors in similar situations have taken decisive steps to improve performance.

Stewart Liff is one such supervisor. When he was appointed Manager at the Veterans Benefits Administration, it was one of the worst performing offices in the country. Stewart turned the office around and made it 30 percent more productive. In the process boosted both client satisfaction and employee morale. How did he do it? He set clear expectations, shared as much information as possible with his employees, and rewarded desired performance. All of this served to create a positive, customer-focused work environment.

b) Meet with employees to identify the causes of the poor performance.

Apply other solutions as outlined in this book.

c) Serve notice that you cannot and will not continue to accept low performance.

d) Recognize that the situation may call for progressive discipline.

Typical steps in a progressive discipline system may include:

1) Counseling low-performing employees on the necessity of improving their performance.

2) Verbally reprimanding them for poor performance.

3) Placing a written warning in their personnel file.

The warning should outline specific steps you will take if performance does not improve.

4) Providing an escalating number of days for them to be suspended from work without pay.

You may want to start with one day and escalate to five.

5) Terminating the individual's employment.

This is obviously a last resort and should not be entered into lightly.

4. Set a positive example.

A survey found that 39 percent of employees thought their supervisor did not set a good example of commitment and passion for the job. Too often, supervisors take a "do as I say; not as I do" approach to leadership. However, most employees will follow your lead whether it is positive or negative. Your attitude and behavior set the tone for the work group. If you hate your job, consistently break the rules and/or goof off, your employees will, too.

Jack, a former supervisor colleague, had decided that, since he only had three more years to work, he really was not interested in putting forth a great deal of effort. Not only that, he made it a point of complaining (in front of his employees) about all the injustices he had endured during his career. As if that were not enough, he also arrived late, regularly took two-hour lunches and was the first one out the door at quitting time. Surprisingly, Jack complained loudly and often about how today's employees were not motivated. Is it any wonder?

Shelly, another supervisor, was always on time, and gave more than an honest day's work. When she asked her employees for long hours of commitment to reach those end–of-month quotas, Shelly was willing to pitch in and support their efforts. Additionally, since she preached ethical behavior and the delivery of quality customer service, she modeled it. Not surprisingly, Shelly's group's performance was far superior to Jack's.

How to set a positive example:

a) Arrive at work before your employees.

This sets the example of punctuality.

b) Keep a positive attitude.

One of my early mentors pointed out that I, as the supervisor, set the tone for the day within the group. He was right. I noticed that when I was in a good mood it gave the employees a boost; when I was not in a good mood it cast a cloud over the entire office. So no matter how crummy a day I was having, I always projected a positive attitude.

c) Carry out your duties diligently.

Keep commitments. Meet deadlines.

d) Follow the rules.

Your employees are much more likely to follow them if they see you doing it.

5. Show your employees that you care about them as people.

"People don't care how much you know until they know how much you care."

– John C. Maxwell, author and consultant

Employees say they want their supervisors to care about them. The want to feel like they are more than just a necessary evil or a tool you are using to meet a quota. However, 57 percent of employees surveyed said their supervisor does not care about them as people. When employees feel that way, they are likely to take the attitude, "If they don't care about me, I don't care about helping them get their results."

Ways to show that you care:

a) Assist with personal problems.

No matter who you are, you will have personal problems. It may be an illness, a problem with a child or a parent, divorce, etc. When these types of things happen to your employees make yourself available to help. One of my employees, Marlene, had been extremely hostile toward me. One day she got sick at work. I drove her home in her car and had another employee follow me to bring me back to the office. As a result, she became one of my best friends and biggest supporters. The other employees mentioned that that single act showed them that they were more than just a means to meeting a customer satisfaction goal each month.

Coach Dick Vermeil of the Kansas City Chiefs has always been known for his human relations skills. He has an open door policy in which players are not only free but are encouraged to come in and talk about anything that is on their minds. It could be a family issue, a relationship issue, or a financial issue. By the way, Dick Vermeil has taken two teams to the Super Bowl and he won 2000.

b) Take some lessons from Southwest Airlines.

They believe:

❑ Their employees are their first customers.

- ❑ You cannot expect your employees to be highly motivated to deliver high quality goods and services if they are not happy.

- ❑ If you treat your employees right, they will treat your customers right.

Among other things, they send cards to all 34,000 employees on their birthday, the anniversary of their employment, on Thanksgiving, and at Christmas.

As a result of their caring attitude toward their employees, Southwest Airlines consistently has the best record among major airlines for on-time performance and for the fewest baggage-handling complaints for the number of customers they carry.

c) Get to know them.

Set aside time to spend with each of your employees to get to know them and their family better.

d) Ask, "How are you?" and actually listen to the answer.

e) Talk about things other than business occasionally.

Employees like talking about what they did on the weekend, what is happening with their children, what's new in their community, what hobbies they have and so on.

f) Print their children's achievements in the organizational newsletter.

Include a picture of both the employee and the child.

g) Help them balance work and family.

According to surveys, 75 percent of employees work more than 40 hours per week. When you add the longer work hours to longer commutes, increased work pressures, demands from family, children, church and community, many workers are struggling to balance all of the heavy demands.

Some ways you can help them balance their life:

1) Allow them to work a flexible schedule.

The majority of employees say they would be happier in their job if they had a more flexible schedule.

2) Permit a daily flex time schedule.

Unlike traditional flex time in which there is a certain set of core hours and the employees can only vary their start and end times, daily flex time enables employees to vary their work hours on a daily basis. This gives them the opportunity to achieve better balance by attending special family events or visiting a doctor during the day. A benefit to the organization, of course, is that you could expand your hours of coverage to meet your clients' needs.

h) Use tactful discipline.

If you have to discipline employees, do it in a way that allows them to maintain their dignity as an adult.

i) Arrange to have a dry-cleaning service pick up employees' dry-cleaning at the office.

It really saves them time if they can drop off and pick up their laundry without making a special trip to the cleaners.

j) Give each employee a copy of *425 Ways to Stretch Your $$$$.*

This was my first book. It offers easy-to-follow tips for saving money on utilities, homeowner insurance, auto insurance, food, credit card bills and many other household expenses. Employees can easily cut their monthly expenses by $1,000.

k) Make the work area attractive and bright.

Employees like to have a pleasant work environment. Get plants and have new lighting installed to brighten up the place. Get the walls painted. Invite a local school to display art. Allow employees to decorate the office.

Figure 19.1

BODY LANGUAGE

Behaviorists who study communication say these are examples of nonverbal message and the meaning they may convey in American culture.

1. FACE

Eye contact

❏ Maintaining eye contact - confidence and interest.

❏ Not maintaining contact - insecurity or lack of interest.

Smile

❏ Satisfaction.

Stroking chin

❏ Trying to make a decision, thinking.

Raised eyebrow

❏ Disbelief, surprise.

Frowning

❏ Disbelief, disagreement, does not understand.

Figure 19.1 - Page 2

BODY LANGUAGE

2. ARMS

Unfolded

- ❑ Openness and honesty.

Folded

- ❑ Defensive, something to hide.

3. HANDS

- ❑ Firm handshake - You are glad to meet them, you are comfortable and confident with the situation.
- ❑ A light wimpy handshake - Lack of interest or insecurity.
- ❑ Making hand gestures - relaxed and confident.
- ❑ Clenched fist – anger or irritation.
- ❑ Hand to cheek – evaluating, thinking.
- ❑ Rubbing hands together – anticipation.
- ❑ Standing with hands on hips – defiant, aggression.
- ❑ Sitting with hands clasped behind head – confidence, superiority.
- ❑ Tapping or drumming fingers – impatience.
- ❑ Rubbing eyes – doubt, disbelief.
- ❑ Rubbing nose – rejection, doubt, lying.
- ❑ Open palm – sincerity, openness, innocence.

Figure 19.1 – Page 3

BODY LANGUAGE

4. HEAD

- Tilted – Interested.

- Leaning forward - Interest.

- Resting in hand – boredom.

- Fast nod – I understand, move on.

- Moderate nod – I think I understand, not sure.

- Slow nod – I understand, but disagree.

- Shaking from side to side
  – disagreement, disbelief.

5. LEGS

- Sitting with legs crossed, foot kicking –
  boredom, nervousness.

- Sitting with legs apart – open, relaxed.

- Brisk, erect walk – confidence.

- Walking with hands in pocket, shoulders
  drooped – dejection.

- Locked ankles – apprehension.

ACTION PLAN

Write any ideas you will implement within your work team.

1. _____.

2. _____.

3. _____.

4. _____.

5. _____.

20

THEY ARE EXPERIENCING PERSONAL PROBLEMS

There could be a pending divorce, child custody issues, demands of aging parents, financial pressures, substance abuse or health problems, just to name a few.

Solution: Develop a plan for helping them deal with the personal problems.

How to implement the solution:

1. Identify the specific problem the employee is having.

I had an employee (Bob) whose performance had deteriorated significantly. I arranged for a quiet place for Bob and me to meet and discuss what was going on with him. During the meeting he said he was experiencing a severe, but yet undiagnosed, medical problem.

2. Explore possible ways of helping the employee solve the problem.

I considered the Employee Assistance Program (EAP) and the medical department.

3. Select a way and implement it.

I referred him to the company medical department. After collecting some basic information from Bob about his symptoms, they arranged for him to see a team of specialists. The specialists diagnosed the problem, began treating him and Bob's performance improved dramatically.

4. Follow up to see if performance improves.

If you have such a situation, you may need to refer the employee to your company/agency medical department or Employee Assistance Program in your company or agency. There may even be some other means of helping, but whatever it is it is up to you (with input from the employee) to find the solution to the personal problem that is causing the performance deficiency.

ACTION PLAN

Write any ideas you will implement within your work team.

1. _____.

2. _____.

3. _____.

4. _____.

5. _____.

INDEX

SUGGESTED READING

Cardy, Robert, *Performance Management*, M.E. Sharp, 2003

Caroselli, Marlene, *Empowerment Works*, American Media Publishing, 1999

Feiner, Michael, *Feiner Points of Leadership*, Warner Press, 2004

Hale, Judith, *Performance-Based Management*, Jossey-Bass, 2003

Harvard Business School Press, *Getting People On Board*, Harvard Business School Press, 2004

Harvard Business School Press, *Motivating People for Improved Performance*, Harvard Business School, 2005

Hawley, Casey, *201 Ways to Turn Any Employee Into A Star Performer*, McGraw-Hill, 2004

Hemsath, Dave, *301 More Ways to Have Fun At Work*, Berrett-Koehler, 2001

Hill, Linda, *Becoming A Manager*, Harvard Business School

Katzenbach, Jon, *Peak Performance*, Harvard Business School Publishing, 2000

Lebedun, Jean, *Managing Workplace Conflict*, American Media, 1998

Lefton, Robert, *Leadership Through People Skills*, McGraw-Hill, 2003

Miller, Brian, *Quick Team-Building Activities for Busy Managers*, Amacon, 2003

Morris, Tom, *The Art of Achievement*, Andrews McMeel Publishing, 2003

Neal, James, *Effective Phrases for Performance Appraisals*, Neal Publications, 2003

Pell, Arthur, *Complete Idiot's Guide to Managing People*, Pearson Education, 1998

Peterson, David, *Leader As A Coach*, PDI, 1996

Rinke, Wolf, *Don't Oil the Squeaky Wheel*, McGraw-Hill, 2004

Silberman, Mel, *The Active Manager's Tool Kit*, McGraw-Hill, 2003

Zeus, Perry, *The Coaching At Work Tool Kit*, McGraw-Hill, 2002

Printed in the United States
58045LVS00003B/154-1008

9 780977 733804